Chaim
WEIZMANN
FIRST PRESIDENT OF ISRAEL

The Yin and the Yang, *an ancient Chinese figure, is symbolic for Century Books, since both negative and positive forces which the figure represents also shape the lives of famous world figures.*

According to folklore, the Yin and the Yang are present in all things, functioning together in perpetual interaction. This balance between opposing forces, and the influences, both good and bad, that have molded the course of history are accurately portrayed as background material in Century biographies.

Chaim WEIZMANN

FIRST PRESIDENT OF ISRAEL

BY RUBY ZAGOREN

A CENTURY BOOK

GARRARD PUBLISHING COMPANY
CHAMPAIGN, ILLINOIS

For
Boris and Hanna Klaz Lenefsky,
my uncle and aunt, the ever-faithful

Acknowledgments:

For reading the manuscript of this book, the author is grateful to Sam E. Bloch, Director of Publications of the Jewish Agency, New York, Rabbi David Korb of Beth El Synagogue, Torrington, Conn., General Ezer Weizmann of Tel Aviv, Elizabeth Graves, Garrard editor, and Samuel Silverstein, Torrington.

Picture credits:

Robert Capa–Magnum: p. 167 (top)
Central Zionist Archives, Jerusalem, Israel: pp. 74, 102 (Yaakov Ben Dov Collection)
Louis Goldman of Rapho Guillumette: p. 159
Radio Times Hulton Picture Library: pp. 37, 64, 87, 120 (both)
United Israel Appeal Archives, Jerusalem, Israel: p. 147
The Weizmann Archives, Rehovoth, Israel: pp. 8 (both), 47, 60, 70, 138 (both)
Yivo Institute for Jewish Research, New York: p. 13
Zionist Archives and Library, New York: pp. 25, 94, 97, 129, 162, 167 (bottom), jacket

Copyright © 1972 by Ruby Zagoren
All rights reserved. Manufactured in the U.S.A.
International Standard Book Number: 8116–4755–2
Library of Congress Catalog Card Number: 74–177893

Contents

1. Childhood in Motol — 7
2. School Days in Pinsk — 18
3. A German Education — 30
4. Student and Teacher in Switzerland — 41
5. A New Face — 49
6. Westward to England — 57
7. The Newlyweds — 66
8. Wartime Chemist — 76
9. The Balfour Declaration — 85
10. Palestine in Wartime — 92
11. Years of Travel — 99
12. The First American Visit — 111
13. Danger Looms — 122
14. Chemist in World War II — 134
15. Let the Gates Open — 145
16. Birth of a Nation — 155

Chronological List of Events in Chaim Weizmann's Life — *171*
Index — *174*

1. Childhood in Motol

The rooster's loud crow rang across Motol, a village in southwestern Russia. Soon other roosters took up the cry, and the village chimed with the lusty crowing.

Ten-year-old Chaim Weizmann, third child of Oser and Rachel, heard that battle cry to face a new day. Under the fluffy feather comforter, he moved closer to his brother, Feivel, who kicked him and mumbled, "Stay in your own place."

How Chaim hated to get up in the cold mornings and step out on the damp, dirt floor. Then he remembered: It was almost Passover, the annual celebration of Jewish freedom. His father might be returning this very day from his long winter of working in the forest.

The house had to be ready for the holiday and for his father's return. The chores had to be finished. This was 1884, but every year events followed the same pattern. Every autumn, right after Sukkot, the harvest festival, Oser Weizmann, a timber merchant, left town with a crew of fifty or sixty moujiks, or peasants. They spent the winter cutting down trees in the deep swamps nearby and sawing them into logs. Winter was the only

Chaim Weizmann (left) lived, as a child, in this house in Motol, a small village in the Russian Pale of Settlement.

time this work could be done. At other seasons, the ground was too soggy and wet. Only when the ground was frozen could the moujiks haul the logs out of the forest.

In the spring when the ice thawed, the logs were floated downstream to cities to be sold. Then the woodcutters and their boss, Oser Weizmann, returned to their families.

With a quick throw of the comforter, Chaim leaped from the warm bed. He struggled into trousers and shirt before the cold air could nip.

"Chaim, go help Yakim feed the chickens," Rachel, his mother, called. Yakim was one of the two peasants who lived with the Weizmanns. They helped Rachel take care of the home, children, and the farm animals during the long months when Oser was away.

"Maria, churn the butter," Rachel called. "Feivel, milk the cow." One by one, Rachel Weizmann summoned her five oldest children to the day's chores.

Chaim knew he should appreciate the chickens. Didn't they provide feathers for the pillows and billowy comforter, and meat for the Sabbath dinner?

On this cold morning, and so early too, Chaim did not appreciate the chickens. He tried to push his hand under the hen's breast to gather the eggs; the tyrant hen nipped him with her sharp beak.

When Chaim finished his chores, he joined his brothers and sisters in the kitchen. There Natasha, the peasant who helped with the housework, prepared breakfast.

"Hurry, you have to go to school," Rachel told them as she brushed one child's hair, then fixed another's collar. "You must not keep the *rebbe* waiting."

"But what if *tatah* comes home? We want to be here," the children protested.

"Enough, enough. You must attend heder. Your father pays a pretty ruble for you to attend classes," Rachel said, and pushed them out the door.

Wrapped in home-knit scarves and looking like bulky dolls, the children headed into the brisk spring wind to walk through Motol's muddy streets.

The heders were the only schools that Chaim and the Jewish children of Motol knew. They did not attend the Russian school, for their parents wanted them to learn the religious traditions and literature of their own people. At the heder, the rebbe, or teacher, spoke in Yiddish, the everyday language of Jews in eastern Europe. The rebbe taught the children, however, to read Hebrew, the language of the ancient Jews in which the Bible had been written.

Like most heders, the one Chaim attended consisted of a single room in the rebbe's house. Here students of all ages sat around the table and studied together. Often in the cruel winter cold, the family goat shared the room with the class. Sometimes the family wash was strung across the classroom to dry, and the rebbe's children, as numerous as the Weizmann offspring, rolled about on the floor and played games.

Chaim had begun going to heder when he was four years old. The *aleph bet,* the ABC's of the Hebrew language, were behind him. Now he studied the Torah, the first five books of the Bible. He also studied the Talmud, a treasury of legends, traditions, and interpretations of biblical laws by numerous Jewish scholars. These books often mentioned the ancient home of the Jewish people, a land hugging the eastern shore of the Mediterranean Sea, where Chaim's ancestors, the people of the Bible, had lived.

Like other ten-year-old heder students, Chaim was well versed in the history of his people and of that faraway land. That part of the world was now called Palestine, but Jews still referred to it in their prayers as Zion, or the land of Israel. They considered it a "holy land."

Here Chaim's ancestors had lived for centuries, sometimes as independent people, sometimes under foreign domination. Then the Romans took control of the Holy Land in the first century B.C. Time after time, the Jews tried to fight off the Roman yoke, but they were never strong enough. Then in 66 A.D., the Roman governor looted the Temple of the Jews in Jerusalem, their sacred city. The Jews rebelled, and for four years they battled huge numbers of well-trained and well-armed Roman soldiers. One by one, the strongholds of the country fell to the Romans until only Jerusalem stood. Finally in 70 A.D., the Romans took Jerusalem too and destroyed the Temple.

The Romans crucified thousands of Jews; they sold others into slavery. Still the remaining Jews rebelled, only to be beaten down by the Romans again. Finally, with a half million dead and at least that number sold into slavery, the Jewish nation was crushed completely. The Romans built a temple to their gods in Jerusalem and gave the country a new name. They called it Palestine.

Although some Jews remained in Palestine, many fled. Some headed east and south across the desert; others managed to get passage on ships and sailed to safer Mediterranean lands. As they scattered across the face of the earth, they took with them their Bible, their traditions, and an abiding faith that somehow, someday, with God's help, they would return to their homeland.

Many Jews settled in Europe. In all countries, they lived peaceably with their Christian neighbors until intolerant leaders or ignorant bigots stirred up trouble. Then the Jews were forced to flee again.

It was probably during one of these troubled periods for Jews that Chaim's ancestors fled from western and central Europe eastward into Poland seeking refuge.

In the 1790s, Poland was partitioned by neighboring countries, and Russia fell heir to a section of the country in which large numbers of Jews, including Chaim's family, lived. Until that time, few Jews had lived in Russia. Now the empress of Russia, Catherine II, suddenly had more than a million Jewish subjects. The empress cruelly restricted the rights of the Jews. They were not protected by Russian law, as were other Poles who had become Russian citizens. And they were not allowed to move out of the newly annexed provinces on Russia's western border.

This area, which extended from the Baltic to the Black Sea, was called the Pale of Settlement. Even in the Pale, however, Jews were not free to live where they wished. Regulations kept them out of certain cities and

Most Russian Jews of the late 1800s lived in close-knit communities in the impoverished towns and cities of the Russian Pale, such as Lubin.

areas. Only in later years did a few Jews obtain permits allowing them to live wherever they wished within the Pale, or in other parts of Russia.

The tsars, who followed Catherine as absolute rulers of Russia and titular heads of the Russian Orthodox Church, were not much kinder. Occasionally a tsar would relax one regulation or another for a short time. In general, however, the Jews living in the Pale of Settlement suffered under all the tsars.

It was in this Pale, in the little town of Motol, that the Weizmann family lived.

Life in Motol was poor and hard. For a Jewish family in Russia, however, the Weizmanns were considered well-off. They owned their own home, a rambling seven-room, one-story house. Their small patch of land allowed them to keep a few chickens and cows.

"There's a lot of living in a cow," Oser Weizmann was fond of saying. The cow gave them a good supply of milk from which they made cheese, yogurt, and butter.

Most important, Oser Weizmann was respected by everyone in the village, by both Jews and Christians. He was the only Jew ever elected headman of the village. In the synagogue, Oser was often asked to lead the prayers to the delight of his children. Oser, who liked to sing, had a beautiful voice.

"I want to sing as well as father does," Chaim often said. He enjoyed learning the traditional songs at heder.

Chaim liked even better those times when the rebbe

interrupted the Bible lesson to talk about other kinds of knowledge.

Most Jews who lived in the narrow world of the Pale were only interested in Jewish learning; they feared that other kinds of knowledge would lead their children away from their religion and traditions.

This rebbe, however, wanted to enlighten his students about the culture and civilization of the modern world, beyond Motol and the Pale. One day he brought to class a textbook, written in Hebrew, about the natural sciences. This textbook had a chapter about a brand-new science called chemistry. The rebbe let his students read aloud certain pages of special interest. Chaim could hardly wait for his turn.

The rebbe knew that the parents were paying him to teach traditional studies, and most of them had never heard about chemistry. Consequently he had Chaim and his other students read the science book in the same chant they used to read ancient Hebrew. Anyone passing by the heder would have heard the chant and never would have suspected that the students were reading anything but the Bible.

Chaim was fascinated with the book. Since Oser Weizmann did not object, Chaim was allowed to take the textbook home one evening. He studied the strange new subject far into the night and hurried to school the next day full of questions. Each day, in fact, he went to school eager to learn.

On the day before Passover, however, Chaim had a hard time keeping his mind on his work. Finally, toward dusk, the rebbe dismissed the students. Chaim and his brothers grabbed their coats and scarves and ran through the streets.

"Is tatah here?" they yelled as they tumbled into their home.

Rachel did not have to answer; she still wore that quiet, resigned look. "Change your clothes, children," she commanded. "Your supper is ready, and there are chores to do. Passover starts tomorrow."

Later that evening, some neighbors stopped by for a short visit. As they sat over their glasses of tea, the conversation, as always, centered on the Holy Land. "Someday our people will return there," an elder said. "Our sages have prophesied."

Chaim listened from his seat in the chimney corner. Afterward, as he lay awake under the comforter, he thought about the Holy Land. Softly Chaim intoned the ancient prayer which he had learned, "If I forget thee, O Jerusalem, let my right hand forget its cunning."

In the silence of the night, Chaim heard a sob. He quietly slid out of bed, pulled his shirt around his shoulders, and stepped into the kitchen. His mother was sitting alone by the dying fire, her hands pressed against her face. Chaim put his arms around her.

"The last part of the waiting is the worst," Rachel said. "A few moujiks have already returned, but your father is responsible for the men and the timber. He's the boss, and he's always the last one home."

In the stillness that followed, Chaim heard a familiar sound. Rachel heard it too. Suddenly she sat up straight. The two looked at each other, then they ran to the window and peered down the dark street. A black shape was moving nearer and nearer. It was a horse-drawn sleigh, and it was coming to their yard.

"It's tatah; it's tatah," Chaim shouted joyfully.

Soon all the Weizmann children woke and tumbled out of bed to greet their father.

Chaim knew this would be a happy Passover. Oser had brought the spirit of the holiday with him. Once again the family would be reunited around the Passover table, and chant together, as Jews had done throughout the centuries, "Next year in Jerusalem."

2. School Days in Pinsk

By the time Chaim was eleven years old, he had completed all the education that the heders of Motol offered. A decision had to be made. Either Chaim could give up schooling altogether and work with his father in the woodlands, or he could do something that no other boy of Motol had ever done. He could enroll at a high school called the Real-Gymnasium in Pinsk, one of the largest cities in the Pale. He would have to leave the bustling warmth of his family and live twenty-five miles away in Pinsk.

Chaim talked this over with his father. It was Oser Weizmann who had first suggested that Chaim, an able student, continue his education.

"You must go to Pinsk," Oser said. "There you will study in Russian schools with Russian students; you will have the benefit of their teachers, their books, and their classes. You will learn many other topics besides Hebrew. Remember how interested you were in your teacher's book about chemistry? In Pinsk you can learn more about chemistry."

"But, father," Chaim argued, "I will be alone there.

No one from Motol has ever gone so far away to study."

"You must go where the school is," Oser said. "Surely you do not expect the Real-Gymnasium to come to Motol."

Chaim still felt uncertain. "But think of the expense," he said. "The tuition, room, and food will cost many rubles. It isn't fair for one son to require all that money."

"For your education I can spare a few rubles," Oser explained. "I want my children to get as much education as possible. That is my dream."

"But . . . ," Chaim began again.

"No more buts," Oser said affectionately and patted Chaim on the shoulder. "You will go to the Real-Gymnasium in Pinsk; it is decided."

Chaim had mixed feelings—he was both happy and sad, proud and afraid, all at the same time.

Oser, noticing his young son's confusion, said tenderly, "Don't worry, Chaim. Someday you will make us all proud of you."

Chaim bit his lip; he felt only smaller and more helpless. He looked so sad that Oser, taking pity, added, "Perhaps Feivel will go with you."

Feivel, three years older than Chaim, was clever at making things with his hands, but he was not as quick a student as Chaim.

Oser now beckoned his eldest son, Feivel, and said, "You, too, shall go to Pinsk. There you will learn a trade and keep Chaim company."

The decision made, Chaim sent an application to the Real-Gymnasium. Feivel was accepted as an apprentice to a lithographer in Pinsk. He would learn the art of printing by drawing letters, pictures, and designs on the flat surface of stones and metals.

How the days raced by, like horses whose driver has lost the reins. Rosh Hashonah and Yom Kippur, the early fall holidays, came and went. It was time to leave home.

Chaim and Feivel bade farewell to their parents, their many brothers and sisters, the family servants, and their friends. As the two boys clambered into the back of the wagon that would carry them to Pinsk, it seemed as though everyone in Motol had gathered to see them off. As the wagon carried them away, Chaim and Feivel kept waving and waving. Only when they could no longer see Motol behind them did the two young brothers turn around and look ahead.

The road to Pinsk was very bumpy. No one ever bothered to rake or smooth the ruts in the dirt road. Chaim and Feivel had to hang onto their seats, or they would have been thrown off when a wheel unexpectedly hit a rock. The boys began to feel sore.

"You can walk a while if you want," the driver said, "but you must keep up with the horse."

The boys jumped off the wagon and jogged alongside until they were winded. Then they climbed back on the wagon to bump along again.

On the way they passed several great estates that contrasted sharply with the dusty, straw-roofed huts of the poor peasants. Even to one as young as Chaim, the great gulf between the rich and poor in Russia was obvious.

Finally, tired and dusty from their long ride, Chaim and Feivel were left at a boardinghouse in Pinsk. Their landlord greeted them, and the driver went off, his horse clopping along the cobblestone street. The boys were shown to their room. It was six feet by four, and contained only a bed and a big pot-bellied stove. The dusty room had an odd smell, and its window opened on a courtyard.

Each morning, after a quick breakfast of bread and milk, the two boys went their separate ways. Feivel went to the lithographer's shop to learn his trade, and Chaim attended classes at the Real-Gymnasium. In the evening, the two brothers had each other to talk to and to confide in.

The boys looked forward to the Sabbath when they went to the synagogue. The Jews of Pinsk greeted them as relatives even though they were strangers.

Chaim found that his new friends trembled whenever they spoke of the pogroms, or massacres, which had taken place a few years before. When Tsar Alexander II was assassinated in 1881, the Jews were blamed for his death. With the encouragement of the new tsar's government, many ignorant villagers and peasants went on a rampage throughout the Pale, killing Jews and looting their homes. The police looked the other way as the defenseless Jews were murdered.

The pogroms had not reached isolated Motol, but these Pinsk Jews had lived through them. They told Chaim and Feivel hair-raising tales of mobs pillaging and burning Jewish homes. They also told the boys of the May Laws passed by the new tsar's government. These laws had decreased the size of the Pale and had turned Russia into a prison for the Jews. The May Laws also limited even further the areas where Jews could live within the Pale.

A few years later new laws would severely restrict the number of Jewish students allowed to attend Russian high schools and universities.

Chaim was fortunate to have started school before these laws made it impossible for more than a handful of Jews to study in Russian schools. True, the teachers at the Real-Gymnasium looked down on Jewish students. After all, the teachers thought, if the tsar approved of pogroms, surely Jews were not the equals of Russians; it was justifiable to treat them as inferiors.

They were mediocre teachers too, Chaim discovered, though they were considered good enough to instruct in a small, provincial town like Pinsk. Chaim, however, did not dwell on the shortcomings of his teachers. Whatever the Russian students were taught, he also was taught.

At first, he had a language problem. In Motol, he had been used to speaking Yiddish and reading Hebrew. But all the books at the Real-Gymnasium were written in Russian. It took a while to become used to that language. By looking up every word he did not know and making it his business to remember them, he soon read Russian fluently.

Each book was like a treasure chest into which he eagerly dipped. The books contained so many facts that he had never heard of before. He learned about people and places in distant lands. He read about a western country named England where people were allowed to live and work as they pleased. Chaim wished Russia had that kind of government.

It was fortunate that Chaim was able to figure out mathematics problems on his own. His teacher knew very little about the subject, and sputtered, coughed, hemmed and hawed whenever he tried to explain the problems. Chaim felt sorry for the mathematics teacher, but he was rascal enough to join his classmates in dreaming up questions to trip him.

When the Real-Gymnasium closed for summer vacation, Chaim and Feivel returned to Motol. After a joyous reunion with his family, Chaim declared, "I must earn some money this summer. It costs father a lot to keep me in Pinsk."

An uncle said, "I have just the job for you. You can sail on my raft as my assistant. We will transport a load of wood up the canal to Brest Litovsk. If you prove worthy, I will let you continue with me down the Boug River to Warsaw."

Chaim grinned. That sounded like a summer of adventure, and he would be earning money at the same time. He eagerly accepted the job.

With a bundle of clothes, Chaim followed his uncle to the nearby stream from which they would leave. On his uncle's raft was a tiny cabin, big enough for a bedroom and a kitchen of sorts. The raft itself was made up of logs lashed together. When they reached their destination, these logs would be unlashed and sold to the highest bidder.

Chaim and his uncle got on the raft and poled downstream. The hours flowed on like the river. Cows came to the water to drink and stare wide-eyed at them. Children ran to play; women kneeled along the edge of the stream to wash their clothes.

Soon they were on the Pina River, approaching Pinsk. How different the town looked from the raft! Chaim pointed out the landmarks to his uncle.

After they passed Pinsk, rain began to fall. The river waters rose steadily.

"We must be extra careful," uncle shouted. "If the current turns the raft sideways, we'll run aground and that could break the ropes that lash the logs together."

The current grew swifter; the shores seemed to race backwards. Chaim and his uncle poled desperately as

A photographer in Pinsk took this picture of the young Chaim when he was a student at the Real-Gymnasium.

they bounced along on the swells and fought the gurgling swirls that tried to push their raft ashore.

After long hours, the rain stopped and the waters settled. Chaim and his uncle relaxed.

"Very good work," his uncle said. "You can make the whole trip with me."

Chaim grinned. They floated on and on. The Pina was connected with the Boug River by a canal; the Boug flowed into the Vistula River. Chaim had never seen such a wide river. Suddenly the raft seemed very small in comparison.

Finally they reached Warsaw, their destination. Chaim stared in amazement at the splendid palaces and the tall cathedrals thrusting their spires upward into the sky.

His uncle sold the raft and its cargo; then it was time to go home. They walked to the railroad station. This was Chaim's first train ride, and he was excited.

The train started with a long, slow chug. As it picked up speed, the countryside glided by. The voyage on the raft had taken weeks. How quickly the train was speeding them home!

Two more years passed by quickly. Chaim studied hard during the winter and spent the summers on his uncle's raft. Then at the beginning of Chaim's fourth year of school, Feivel returned to Motol. There wasn't enough money this year to pay for boarding both boys in Pinsk, so Feivel would have to stay home and help his father with the timber.

Chaim grew used to living alone in Pinsk. He made friends with some of his schoolmates, and one teacher took an interest in him. His name was Mr. Kornienko, and he taught chemistry. All by himself, Mr. Kornienko had put together a small laboratory, an unheard-of innovation in most Russian high schools of that time. Here in this makeshift laboratory, with only a few test tubes and one burner, Mr. Kornienko allowed Chaim and his other good students to experiment.

What fun it was for Chaim to take part in the experiments Mr. Kornienko performed! He loved science and listened intently as the teacher pointed out chemical changes in iron that rusted, or in coal that burned and changed into ash, water vapors, and gases.

It was easy for Chaim to see that Mr. Kornienko was an outstanding teacher. He was unusual in other ways too, for he treated the Jewish students as kindly as he treated his Russian students.

After school, Chaim often visited some of the Jewish families in Pinsk. He joined the "Lovers of Zion," a new organization which was raising money to buy land in Palestine and to send young Jewish immigrants there. Unlike the elderly Jews who had trickled back to the Holy Land over the years to spend their last days there, these young people hoped to establish farming colonies. The "Lovers of Zion" had to meet secretly because Zionism, as this movement was called, was illegal in Russia.

These meetings reminded Chaim of home. The older people sat and chatted and dreamed aloud while the younger ones, like Chaim, listened.

One night at a "Lovers of Zion" meeting, Chaim was thrilled to learn that a Pinsk youth named Aaron Eisenberg was actually leaving for Palestine. There he would join other pioneers in farming the land and planting trees.

To Chaim, Aaron seemed like the biblical David going to face an unknown Goliath. Farming would be difficult, Chaim knew, for through the centuries, Palestine had suffered again and again at the hands of conquerors who had cut down the forests for fuel and used up the good soil. Some of these conquerors swept through the Holy Land because of its strategic importance, others because of its religious significance. For over the years, Palestine had become the Holy Land for several religious faiths.

Christians revered Palestine because it was here that Jesus had grown to manhood and preached his message. Later, about the time that the Roman Empire fell, a young Arab named Mohammed founded another religion, called Islam; this new religion was based partly on the Jewish Bible and partly on the teachings of Jesus. In the seventh century, Moslems, as the followers of Islam were called, rode out of the Arabian desert and conquered Palestine. They built the Mosque of Omar in Jerusalem; now the Holy Land was sacred to Moslems as well as to Jews and Christians.

Some 500 years slid through the hour glass. Christian Crusaders journeyed from Europe to try to take control of the Holy Land from the Moslems. The Crusaders eventually won and ruled the country for 150 years. Then a Moslem named Saladin swept out of the desert and captured the land.

In 1516, other Moslems from Turkey, called Ottomans, fought and won the Holy Land. Ever since then Turkey had ruled Palestine. Turkey had little concern for conditions there. Now in 1890, the neglected country was a wasteland. Cities had crumbled; rains had washed away the soil from the treeless mountains; swamps filled many of the valleys; and malarial mosquitoes bred in the marshes. The population of this forsaken land was barely 300,000. Of this number, only 25,000 were Jews.

If Aaron were brave enough to go to Palestine, Chaim wanted to help him. When the "Lovers of Zion" decided to take up a collection to pay some of Aaron's expenses, Chaim volunteered to canvass the town.

In an overcoat that swept the ground—his mother made it long so Chaim could get extra wear in case he grew taller—Chaim tramped through the Pinsk streets.

One family gave a kopeck; another gave five kopecks; one gave a ruble. The Pinsk Jews, each according to his means, were happy to help send Aaron to the Holy Land. More than once, Chaim tripped on his long overcoat and fell headlong into the icy slush on the street. When he finally turned in his collections, he watched as the elders counted them, kopeck by kopeck.

"You collected more than anyone else," one of the elders announced. Then he smiled, "Chaim Weizmann, you are sending a little of yourself with Aaron to the Holy Land."

Chaim beamed as he heard the praise. The rabbi had expressed his desire exactly. The time and energy spent in collecting the money was his investment in Aaron's journey. Perhaps someday he would go in person to the Holy Land.

3. A German Education

After seven years in Pinsk, Chaim graduated from the Real-Gymnasium at the top of his class. He was eighteen and once again had to make a decision. He could go to work and help support the family, which now consisted of twelve children, or he could continue with his education.

Again he discussed the situation with his father.

"Somehow you must continue your studies," Oser said, stroking his beard. "But such a small number of Jews are allowed to attend the Russian universities that I'm afraid you might not be admitted."

"You're right," Chaim said gloomily. "I might not place high enough in the special entrance examinations that we Jews must take. They are five times harder than those given the Russians. And even if I do pass, the police might not give me a permit to live outside the Pale."

"Sometimes the universities sell admission to the highest bidder," Oser said, "but I don't have enough money to compete."

"Why can't I go west?" Chaim asked. "Lots of Jews have gone to Germany to study."

"That's a good idea," Oser nodded, "a very good idea."

Soon afterward the Weizmanns heard of a Jewish boarding school in Pfungstadt, Germany, which was looking for a junior teacher. Chaim applied for the position and, in time, was accepted.

He would tutor students in Hebrew and Russian for two hours a day. In exchange, he would earn his room, board, and 300 marks—about $75—for the year. In his free time, he could study at the University of Darmstadt, less than an hour from Pfungstadt by train.

"This solves the problem," Chaim exulted. "With my earnings, I should be able to pay most of my fees and buy my books."

He began studying the German language. He found it so similar to Yiddish that he learned it easily.

It was heartwarming to know he had a job and could continue his studies. Now he had to figure out how to get to Pfungstadt. It was 1892, a time when no Russian Jew could travel without an identification card. In addition, he needed a foreign passport, a very expensive document.

"I've got just enough money to reach Pfungstadt fourth class," Chaim figured. "I don't have money for the passport."

His uncle, the rafter, heard about his problem. "Why worry about a passport?" his uncle asked. "As a raft worker, you can float to Germany free of charge." He laughed.

"It isn't legal," Chaim protested.

"Are the Russian laws fair to us Jews?" his uncle answered.

So once again Chaim became his uncle's assistant. Chaim did his share of the work until they reached Thorn, the first German port. There he picked up his bundle of clothes and left the raft. He found his way to the railroad station and took the first train to Pfungstadt.

Once there, Chaim plunged into an exhausting schedule. Every morning he got up at five to catch the train to Darmstadt. He arrived at 6:30 A.M., but the university did not open for another hour, so he walked the streets to keep warm. He carried a roll and a piece of cheese for lunch; he had no money to spend on extra food. After classes, he returned to Pfungstadt by 4:30 P.M., and taught students for two hours. After a meager supper, he studied until late nearly every night.

Chaim was not happy at Pfungstadt. He missed the warmth of the Russian Jews, who took pride in their traditions. The Pfungstadt headmaster admired Germany's leadership in science and culture and thought of himself as completely German in every way except for his religion, which was Jewish.

Chaim, since his arrival, had observed his fellow students carefully. One night, during supper, Chaim said, "I think the Germans hate Jews."

"And the Russians love Jews?" the headmaster retorted.

"The Russians hate us, and we know it," Chaim said. "But here in Germany, Jews don't realize how the Germans feel about them."

The headmaster nodded solemnly and said, "We must not take the hatred seriously. If some Germans don't like Jews, it's because they do not know our sterling qualities. They have to be told."

Chaim wondered if the headmaster were right. As the weeks went by, he saw that German Jews were given few opportunities to serve in the government. Those Jews who were allowed to put the honorary "von" before their names had to be baptized as Christians first. Chaim felt that the German Jews were trading their self-respect for an empty honor.

The headmaster repeated, "If the Germans are told about the sterling qualities of the Jews, they will understand our worth."

Chaim exploded. He knew that the Germans hated Jews and would continue to hate them no matter how often they were reminded of their good qualities. "Herr Doctor," he raged, "if a man has something in his eye, he doesn't want to know whether it's mud or gold. He just wants to get it out."

The headmaster, who demanded strict obedience from his teachers as well as his students, was speechless with anger. After that, he glared every time he saw Chaim.

Chaim managed to last through that year. The chemistry classes were so engrossing that he forgot about his hungry, grumbling stomach. Finally the long hours and the lack of food caught up with him. By the time he returned home, after only two semesters, he was in poor health.

Home for the Weizmanns was now in Pinsk. With six children attending the Real-Gymnasium, Oser found it easier on his finances to move close to the school. He could take care of his timber business as easily in Pinsk as in Motol.

This year the timber business was in a slump. It was hard to find customers. Oser could not scrape together enough money to send Chaim back to the university. Chaim did not want to return to Pfungstadt anyway. Once he regained his health, he found a job in a small chemical factory in Pinsk. He remained at home with his family for a year.

During the year, Maria, Chaim's older sister, married, and her husband went into business with Oser. The price of timber was rising, and so Oser encouraged Chaim to return to his studies.

"I hear the Berlin Polytechnium has the best chemistry professors," Oser told Chaim. "If you are admitted to the Polytechnium, I want you to go there."

Chaim applied and was accepted.

"You won't have to work this time," Oser said. "I can give you an allowance. That should spare your health."

Once again Chaim traveled west. In Berlin, he found hundreds of other young Jewish students from Russia; he felt at home with them.

He devoted himself to his chemistry. What luxury to have the entire day for classes and homework! Chaim became fascinated with dyes. At first he followed formulas devised by other chemists to produce different colors. He used coal tars to make a variety of lovely hues. As he gained more experience and confidence, Chaim tried his own formulas. He began experimenting with such coal tars as benzene, naphthalene, and anthracene on his own, to see what synthetic dyes he could make. It was an exciting time.

Chaim joined an organization called the Jewish–Russian Scientific Society. He found, in this group, young men who shared his interests in both science and the Jewish destiny.

Chaim was in his second year at the Polytechnium when a new book stirred him and other Jews throughout the world. Theodor Herzl, a Hungarian Jew and a journalist, who was unknown to Chaim and the other students, published *The Jewish State*.

In this book Herzl urged Jews to stop dreaming and to start planning practical ways of establishing a Jewish state. Herzl, Chaim learned, had only recently become aware of the extent of anti-Jewish feeling in Europe. Herzl had been a reporter at a trial in France where Captain Alfred Dreyfus, a Jewish officer in the French army, was wrongfully convicted of selling military secrets to the Germans.

Herzl was shocked at the anti-Jewish feelings expressed at this trial in a democratic country. He came to believe that Jews would never be treated as equals anywhere until they had a country of their own where they could govern themselves.

After reading *The Jewish State*, Chaim and his fellow students could talk of nothing else.

"What daring that Herzl has!" Chaim exclaimed. "What energy! Others have had the idea of a Jewish state before, but no one has presented the idea so dramatically."

Soon Chaim learned that Herzl was starting negotiations with the sultan of Turkey to buy acreage in the Holy Land for the entire Jewish people. Since it was against Turkish law for any Jew to purchase land in Palestine, those Jews who had immigrated there in recent years had been forced to buy land illegally from individual owners. Herzl hoped to end this situation.

Shortly afterward Chaim heard that Herzl was calling for the creation of a Zionist Congress. He set the date of the first meeting for the late summer of 1897 in Basel, Switzerland.

Chaim and the other students were ecstatic.

"This is a public declaration," Chaim said. "Jews are reasserting their existence; they are confronting humanity with their historic demands."

Theodor Herzl

"You are carried away," one of the students laughed.

Chaim, however, was serious. "We must make sure this first Zionist Congress is a success. Everyone has to help. We students have to help too."

"That's true," the students agreed. "If Herzl can call a Zionist Congress, we can make sure all the Jews are represented."

Chaim and many of his friends decided to spend their summer vacation visiting Jews throughout Russia. "The least we can do is tell them about the Congress and get them to send delegates."

As soon as the Polytechnium closed for the summer,

the Jewish students rushed home. Chaim spent his entire vacation going from one community to another, spreading the news about the first Zionist Congress. Sometimes he had to walk miles from one village to another; sometimes he paddled a boat through dismal swamps to reach remote settlements. Everywhere he urged the Jews to send delegates.

When he spoke to the Jews in Pinsk, they elected him as one of their representatives. Chaim felt well rewarded for his work.

Before Chaim could attend the Congress, however, he had to visit Moscow. During the past year at the Polytechnium, he had created a new dye. His professor felt Chaim could sell the formula, and had given him the name of the manager of a Moscow dyeing plant. Chaim liked the idea of earning some money from his beloved experiments. Besides, the money would pay for his trip to the Zionist Congress.

Chaim applied for an official permit to travel outside the Pale. When the police turned down his request, he was left with no choice. He had to travel secretly, and he could not stay at hotels because the police checked records.

Chaim made his plans in advance. He wrote to his Jewish friends who were permitted to live in Moscow; they agreed to let him sleep in their rooms. Of course, if his friends were found out, they could be arrested too.

Chaim rode on a load of vegetables to the edge of the

Pale. During the night, he managed to cross the boundary safely, and soon found another ride. The trip seemed endless. Chaim could not relax; he felt the police might find him at any moment.

Once in Moscow, he went directly to the dye works office. He was kept waiting several hours, and then was told to return the next morning. Chaim grew more fidgety. The trip was taking much longer than he planned. When the manager finally saw Chaim, he did not buy Chaim's formula, because it was a bad year for the dye business.

Disappointed, Chaim headed home. "I didn't sell my formula," Chaim told his father. "I can't afford to go to the Congress after all."

"I would like to help you, but I can only spare ten rubles right now," Oser said sadly.

"Oh, father, I didn't realize how poor business is this year. I can't take any more money from you," Chaim cried. "You pay my tuition; that's enough."

"But you worked so hard for the Congress," Oser said.

"I won't go this time," Chaim answered. "Surely there will be a second Zionist Congress."

Chaim spent a couple of quiet weeks at home, and then returned to the Berlin Polytechnium. The students who had attended the Congress told him about the program adopted there: "The object of Zionism is to establish for the Jewish people a publicly and legally assured home in Palestine."

This news excited Chaim. For the first time in 2,000 years, the Jews had spoken as if they really meant to return to the Holy Land.

The delegates at the first Zionist Congress had discussed constructing a Hebrew university in Jerusalem and creating a Jewish bank. They had adopted a design for a national flag: a six-pointed blue star on a white background, since blue and white were the colors of the traditional prayer shawl. A Hebrew song, "Hatikvah," meaning "hope," was chosen as the national anthem.

Most important, Chaim felt, was that the Congress had endorsed Herzl's aim of building a Jewish nation.

Chaim sighed. How he wished he had been at the Congress.

"People asked for you," one student told Chaim. "Delegates from the communities you visited wanted to know where you were."

Chaim smiled a small smile. He had missed that first Congress, but he would make sure he attended the next one. Meanwhile he consoled himself by singing over and over to himself the words of "Hatikvah":

> *Our ancient hope will not perish,*
> *Hope from ages long since past.*
> *To live free in the land we cherish,*
> *Zion and Jerusalem, at last.*

4. Student and Teacher in Switzerland

During the next year, Chaim kept informed of Herzl's work. Herzl was traveling to European capitals in an effort to awaken interest among world leaders in Jewish self-rule. He had scheduled the second Zionist Congress for late August 1898, in Basel, Switzerland.

"I am going this time," Chaim told his father when he went home for summer vacation. "I've saved enough money for my expenses. I will attend the Congress and then return to the Polytechnium."

Chaim looked forward to meeting Herzl personally. When the second Congress opened in Basel, Chaim was there. Herzl presided at the meetings. He was not very tall, but there was something arresting about this intense man with a black, square cut beard and glowing deep set eyes. He dominated the Congress with his extraordinary personality, his dramatic gestures, and his ardor. Chaim thought the ancient prophets might have looked and spoken as Herzl did.

Chaim Weizmann, one of the youngest delegates, also impressed the Congress with his friendly smile and the simplicity of his speech. He urged the Congress to take definite steps to make the dream of a university in Jerusalem come true.

Chaim was pleased when the second Zionist Congress established a bank, the Jewish Colonial Trust in London. It was supported by thousands of small stockholders, who were happy to invest in the possibility of a Jewish homeland.

Chaim had never felt as happy as he did at the Congress. "For me this was a time of undiluted joy and spiritual happiness," he would write later. "In these surroundings, I felt at home; I felt welcome, and I felt myself to be needed."

As soon as the Congress ended, Chaim went on to Berlin; there he completed his third year at the Polytechnium. Then his favorite chemistry professor left to take a position at the University of Freiburg. Chaim wanted to continue studying under that professor, so he transferred to the Swiss university for his final year.

When it was time for graduation, Oser and Rachel came to Freiburg for the ceremonies. Chaim saw his parents beaming as he walked past them in the academic procession. Oser and Rachel smiled even more proudly when Chaim was awarded the degree of Doctor of Science with the highest distinction, *summa cum laude*.

Afterward, Oser put his arm around Chaim and said, "I am pleased, son."

"You're the one who should be getting the honors,"

Chaim said, glancing at the sheepskin in his hand. "You made it possible."

"Your honors are my reward," Oser said. "Besides, your success will spur your brothers and sisters on to study harder."

"They're following your footsteps," Rachel added. "We have two in heder now, and four or five—or is it six—at the Real-Gymnasium, and one starting at the university."

Chaim told his parents that his honors had won him a position at the University of Geneva. He would be a *privat docent*, assistant lecturer in chemistry, a position that offered no fixed salary. He would receive 50 marks per pupil for each term. Chemistry was comparatively new then and attracted few students.

"My income will be meager," Chaim told his parents over a glass of tea, "but the position is the first rung on the ladder of university teaching. Besides, I will have the use of a laboratory."

"It's a good place to begin," Oser agreed.

When Chaim Weizmann, the young lecturer, arrived in Geneva, he was delighted with the beauty of the blue lake that mirrored snowcapped Mt. Blanc and the other Alpine peaks. He looked up at the peaks and remembered the ancient psalm, "Lift thine eyes to the mountains whence cometh strength."

Once classes began, the young lecturer described chemistry to his students as "an unfolding world of endless possibilities." He showed how "through the combination of various elements, man can expand his universe." He described the new products that chemistry was creating and exhibited the new synthetic dyes he himself had produced. He invited the students into his private laboratory to watch his experiments.

His own research now helped support him. Germany's I.G. Farbenindustrie purchased one of his discoveries in dyestuff chemistry. Shortly afterward, a Paris firm purchased still another patent.

"This is a stroke of marvelous luck," Chaim Weizmann told his colleagues. "Money isn't important when you have enough, and I will now have plenty."

Dr. Weizmann sent a generous amount home to help his father pay tuition fees for his brothers and sisters.

To relax in the evening, he often walked to the popular Café Landolt where the students gathered to sip tea from glasses and to chat. He made a habit of seeking out the Jewish students from Russia and discussing Zionism, Herzl, and Jewish aspirations with them.

When he spoke to these students about a future homeland, Dr. Weizmann found there in Geneva other Russians who were dissatisfied with life at home. They yearned to overthrow the tsar and reform the Russian government and economy.

Geneva, he found, was the crossroads of Europe's revolutionaries, and served as a refuge for political agitators who had fled from arrest in their own countries.

A young Italian named Benito Mussolini was there, but Dr. Weizmann was much more concerned about a young Russian, Vladimir Ilyitch Lenin, the leader of a group of radical Socialists, later known as Communists. Lenin wanted the Russian-Jewish students to join his group.

Lenin had studied law in Russia, Dr. Weizmann learned, but he had never practiced seriously. Instead, he had become a professional revolutionary, dedicated to the overthrow of the Russian monarchy. Dr. Weizmann heard how Lenin had been jailed and exiled to Siberia. Lenin had escaped and was now in Geneva, where he edited a revolutionary newspaper.

Dr. Weizmann worried when he heard that Lenin was trying to win the support of the Russian-Jewish students. "Throw in your lot with me," Lenin shouted. "We will establish a classless society in Russia, and you Jews will be treated like everyone else."

Weizmann knew that Russia had nurtured hatred of the Jews for many generations and that hatred would not die overnight, despite Lenin's promises. He feared that the students would be swayed by the words of the Russian revolutionist.

Dr. Weizmann was also concerned when he heard George Plekhanov, a friend of Lenin and a teacher of Russian Marxism, trying to discredit the Zionist movement. Plekhanov declared that Jews who believed in a national future for their people were "intellectually backward, chauvinistic, stupid, and immoral."

What could Dr. Weizmann do? Lenin had an organization and followers, and he spoke convincingly. The Jewish students had no organization and no leaders.

Dr. Weizmann decided he had to do something. He scheduled a meeting at which Jewish students could discuss their problems. He rented the back room of the Russian Colony Library and tacked notices up in the Café Landolt and on the university bulletin board.

The Jews were not the only ones who read the notices. Lenin and Plekhanov read them too. They did not want the Jews to hold this meeting. Just before it was to start, they sent some of their followers to the library. They removed every chair from the room. Lenin and Plekhanov reasoned that nobody would stay for a meeting if he could not sit down.

Dr. Weizmann went to the library at the appointed time. He was astonished to see the empty room, but it was too late to cancel the meeting.

"Where are the chairs?" the first students to arrive asked.

"Chairs or no chairs, this meeting must be held," Weizmann declared. "You can stand up, can't you?"

The students agreed. They jammed into the room, and, before they left, they had formed the first Zionist Society of Switzerland.

Lenin was furious. He pounded the table in his room with his fist and cried to his friends, "The Jews must not do this. We Russians must stick together." Lenin and

A serious Chaim (center) posed in Geneva with some of his friends. Martin Buber is seated at the right.

Plekhanov went to the cafés and told the Jewish students, "Zionist work is impractical; you have no land; you never will. Throw in your lot with us."

Worried over this increased attention to the Jewish students, Dr. Weizmann scheduled a second meeting. He invited Martin Buber, a brilliant young writer, to come from Berlin and speak.

On the appointed night, Chaim Weizmann and Martin Buber arrived at the Russian Colony Library early. The chairs were in place. Weizmann paced up and down the room as he wondered whether the students would attend. He was just about convinced that no one was coming when two students arrived and sat down. Soon a few more drifted in. By the time Martin Buber got up to speak, the room was crowded. Buber talked about Herzl and the accomplishments of the Zionist Congress. Afterward, the young people crowded around Weizmann and Buber to ask questions.

This second meeting angered the Russian Socialist leaders more than the first. Plekhanov stalked into Weizmann's laboratory. The young lecturer turned off the Bunsen burner and nodded a greeting.

Plekhanov began shouting, "You are splitting our ranks. It's far more important that we have a revolution in Russia than for you stiff-necked Jews to meddle and muddle with your puny ambitions. You'll never own Palestine; I won't let you."

Chaim Weizmann drew himself up, looked Plekhanov in the eye, and said, "You sound just like the tsar."

Plekhanov sputtered, shot a look of hatred at Weizmann, turned, and slammed the door as he left.

To counteract the growing activities of Lenin and Plekhanov, Dr. Weizmann organized two additional Zionist societies in Switzerland—one in Berne, another in Zurich. Because he could not attend all the meetings personally, he started a newspaper and wrote articles to inspire the students. He got other people, such as Martin Buber, to write for the newspaper too.

Teaching chemistry, doing research, and publishing the newspaper kept Chaim Weizmann busy from early morning until late at night.

5. A New Face

One afternoon, after Chaim had finished his laboratory work and checked his students' experiments, he decided to stop at Café Landolt for a bowl of sour cream and some dark bread.

As he entered the café, he noticed a group of girls who, he felt sure, had just arrived from Russia. Many Jewish girls came to Geneva to study for the same reason—they could not gain admittance to universities in Russia. Chaim Weizmann was particularly attracted to one pretty girl with curly black hair, the quietest in the group. She seemed to have a faraway look as though she were either pensive or sad.

Chaim struck up a conversation with the girls. "I'm Chaim Weizmann," he said. "I want to welcome you to Geneva."

The pretty, pensive girl said her name was Vera Chatzman from Rostov-on-Don, Russia. She was studying medicine, she told him shyly.

"Perhaps I will see you at this café again," the lecturer said.

She smiled a tiny smile at the tall, balding man. She was impressed by his finely modeled head, and by the strength and the kindness in his face. "I am sure I will come here again," she said.

From time to time, Chaim and Vera chatted over a glass of Russian tea at the café. Sometimes they attended concerts, as they shared a love of music. Sometimes they strolled around the lake.

Their friendship developed slowly, for they were both aware of the differences between them. He was a lecturer and a mature man; she was a young student of nineteen. They also found that, although both came from Russia, their lives had been entirely different. He had grown up in the Pale; she was brought up in Rostov, outside the Pale, where her father had been given special permission to live because of his military service. She had been spared many of the humiliations Chaim had experienced.

Their attitudes toward their Jewish heritage were also different. He, of course, was an ardent Zionist. Vera knew very little about Zionism or about Jewish problems inside or outside of Russia.

"I am more interested in my studies than in politics," she commented. "Some students spend so much time arguing that they forget they came here to study."

Sometimes Chaim became exasperated with her attitude. One day he asked, "How can an intelligent girl like you be so ignorant of the Zionist movement?"

Challenged, Vera said, "Tell me then exactly what Zionism is."

Chaim spent several hours describing the history of the movement, Herzl, and the Zionist Congresses.

When he had finished, she asked, "But, Chaim, how do I know that what you say is right?"

He took a deep breath. "You must think about it for yourself and find your own answers. I cannot say any more."

Chaim escorted her in silence to the house where she was lodging. Before they parted, he said, "I will loan you a few books on Zionism. I want you to read Herzl's *The Jewish State.*"

Vera said, "I'll promise to read the book, but I may not agree with you anyway."

During that year, they discussed Zionism frequently, but although attracted to each other, they did not speak of a future together.

Vera continued to read about Zionism. As she listened to Chaim, she came to understand that Zionism was as much a part of Chaim Weizmann as his eyes and ears. As Vera learned more about Zionism, she slowly began to agree with its philosophy.

Nearly three years went by before Chaim and Vera decided to marry. Even then they knew that they would have to wait another three years until Vera completed her studies and Chaim felt confident enough of his finances to take on the responsibility of marriage.

In the winter of 1903, news reached Chaim that the tsar was sending thousands of young Jews to exile in Siberia. Chaim was upset as he told Vera about this new persecution.

"This is the twentieth century, and Jews are no longer bearing their humiliations in silence," Chaim declared. "Some are joining the revolutionaries, and some are joining the Zionists. Both groups are illegal in Russia. The police have been arresting people whom they suspect of membership in these movements."

"I've noticed a great many new Jewish students in the cafés," Vera said. "Some of them talk of friends who are leaving for America."

"Jews are going wherever they can," Chaim said, "for they know that there is little hope for them in Russia." He shook his head. "I can't help worrying about my family."

When Passover came, Chaim Weizmann visited his family in Pinsk, and then went on to Warsaw to consult older Zionist leaders. While there, he heard the chilling news of a pogrom in Kishinev, a town in the Pale of Settlement. Dr. Weizmann learned that forty-five men, women, and children had been killed by Russian mobs. Almost another thousand were injured. The police had stood by and had done nothing to protect the victims.

Weizmann hurried east to the Pale. Again he walked from town to town, or paddled a small boat through the swamps to reach remote settlements. This time he helped the Jews organize self-defense groups. He told each family, "You must get weapons and hide them in your homes. The Kishinev pogrom proves that the Russian police will not help you. You can rely on no one but yourselves."

When another pogrom broke out near Pinsk, the hoodlums were in for a surprise. When they began attacking the Jews, the Jews defended themselves. For the first time the Jews had fought back.

In August, Chaim Weizmann traveled to Basel for the sixth Zionist Congress. There he learned that the entire civilized world had been aroused by the Kishinev massacre. England, in fact, was offering Herzl the Uganda territory in British East Africa for a Jewish homeland.

When Herzl announced this offer from the speakers' platform, Chaim Weizmann could feel the excitement run through the crowd. For the first time in nearly 2,000 years, a world power had communicated with the representatives of the Jewish people, and that world power had also offered them land!

As Weizmann and other delegates began considering the Uganda offer, their excitement died down.

"What is Uganda to us?" they argued. "We are not interested in Uganda; we have our roots in Palestine. Palestine was the land of our ancestors, the land of the Bible. We don't want any other land."

Still others declared, "We must not offend the British

by refusing. Besides, how long can we wait for the sultan of Turkey to sell us a tract of land in Palestine? Uganda will give our persecuted brethren a place of refuge now."

Chaim Weizmann argued the longest against Uganda. He stood before the Congress and told the delegates, "Zionism for me is more than a movement to find a home for oppressed Jews. Rather, for me, Zionism is the whole of Jewishness, a unifying spiritual force."

Chaim Weizmann paced up and down the platform as he spoke. "We Jews," he continued, "must return to the land of our fathers, free intellectually as well as physically; we must speak our own language, renew our culture, and develop our spiritual heritage."

He paused and turned to face the delegates as he stated, "Uganda is not for us; we have no roots there. The forces on which Zionism is based lie deep in the psychology of our people and in its living impulses. We know that Palestine cannot be obtained in short order. If the British government and people are what I think they are, they will make us a better offer. They will help us get Palestine."

The delegates who agreed with Chaim Weizmann cheered as he left the platform. The debate and speeches went on for nearly three days. Finally the time came to vote. Every delegate had to answer "yea" or "nay" when his name was called.

Every "yea" seemed like a hammer blow to Chaim

Weizmann and his followers, and a wail of sorrow rose. All around the hall men stood weeping. Family bonds and lifelong friendships were shattered as the delegates voted.

Chaim Weizmann led one group of delegates in a storm of "nays." Then he bit his lip as he heard his father and his brother Shemuel vote "yea."

Next came the roll call of the Kishinev delegates who had lived through the pogrom. The two men arose and shouted, "Nay, the Holy Land or nothing!"

Theodor Herzl was amazed. "Those Jews from Kishinev... they have a rope around their necks, and still they refuse."

When the vote was tallied, the Zionist Congress had decided 295 to 175 to accept the Uganda offer, but 100 delegates had not voted at all. There were not enough "yea" votes for the proposition to be put into effect at that time.

Chaim Weizmann and the other "nay" voters got up and marched out of the hall. They went to a hotel room to discuss their hopes for the Holy Land, but no one felt like speaking. They sat there depressed. Some were crying; some were fuming; some sat on the floor mourning as people mourn their dead.

A message arrived. Herzl wanted to speak to them. Chaim Weizmann invited Herzl in. Herzl, looking haggard and exhausted, entered the room. He was received in silence. Nobody rose to greet him. He admonished them for leaving the hall and pleaded with them to return to the Congress. Herzl assured them again that his interest in Uganda was only as a temporary refuge and that he had not deserted the idea of a Jewish state in Palestine.

Before he left, Herzl raised his right hand and repeated the awesome biblical pledge: "If I forget thee, O Jerusalem, let my right hand forget its cunning." Then Herzl left as he had entered, in silence.

Chaim Weizmann considered a few more minutes, then followed Herzl back to the hall. He knew that the hope for a homeland still lay in the Congress.

When the Zionist Congress drew to a close, Weizmann wondered if he had voted correctly. He really did not know anything about Uganda. He decided to visit England and to find out for himself about Uganda and the English offer.

In London, he interviewed a noted explorer who had been in Uganda. The explorer told him that Uganda had an extremely hot climate; its land was overgrown with bush, and both the natives and the English settlers there would fight if anyone tried to take their land.

Next, Weizmann talked with an English statesman who said, "If I were a Jew, I would not give a halfpenny for the Uganda proposition."

Chaim Weizmann was now convinced beyond all doubt that he had voted in the best interests of his people.

6. Westward to England

Chaim Weizmann took a train from London to Dover, where he boarded the ferry to cross the English Channel. He turned and looked back at the white chalk cliffs of Dover.

As the ferry rose and fell with the rough waters, he remembered Herzl once remarking that England had sympathy for the Zionist cause. He remembered, too, that England had once had a Jewish prime minister, Benjamin Disraeli.

Back in Geneva, he told Vera, "Switzerland is beautiful, perhaps the most beautiful country in the world, but I feel I belong in England."

"Why?" she asked. "We don't manage to see each other as much as we'd like, even when you are in Geneva. Why go to England, Chaim?"

"I've devoted so much time to Zionism, Vera, that I have neglected my profession," Chaim answered. "I'd like to concentrate on chemistry for a while, and I think it will be easier to do so in England. But I won't make the move until next year. When you finish your studies, we will marry and you can join me in England."

"I can't imagine your losing interest in Zionism," Vera said.

"I won't," Chaim said. "I have the feeling that the road to the Holy Land runs through England."

The academic year soon passed. Chaim Weizmann planned to leave Geneva on July 4, 1904. He was packing the last of his books when a telegram arrived.

He tipped the messenger and stood in the open doorway as he ripped open the envelope. His eyes must be playing tricks on him, he felt. The telegram said that Theodor Herzl was dead.

Herzl was only forty-four years old, but a saddened Chaim knew that the Uganda issue had worn him out. The sixth Congress with its passionate debates, extra work, and long hours had left Herzl's imposing figure sagging with weariness.

Wondering what the course of Zionism would be without Herzl, Chaim Weizmann set out for England to embark on a new life. He had a letter of introduction to Professor William Henry Perkin, the head of the Chemistry Department at Victoria University in Manchester.

Chaim hoped that Professor Perkin would be able to help him find a position. Manchester itself was the center of England's chemical industry.

When Weizmann met Perkin, he was delighted to find that the professor could speak fluent German. They were able to communicate freely.

"The university is closed for the summer," Perkin said, "but if you would like to use a laboratory for your own research, I am sure it can be arranged."

Weizmann was delighted and accepted the offer immediately. He found lodgings and moved in.

The laboratory turned out to be a dingy, dusty basement room that had not been used in some time. During his first day there, Chaim Weizmann did what any good housekeeper would do. He rolled up his sleeves and scrubbed. He scrubbed the tables and the sinks. He scrubbed the apparatus and the test tubes. He got down on his hands and knees to scrub the floor. By the end of the day, his knees ached.

"I've got housemaid's knee," he wrote to Vera.

With his laboratory clean and shining, he was ready to begin further experimentation on synthetic dyes. Day after day he worked long, hard hours. He tried one formula and then another; he tried different combinations of such substances as benzene, naphthalene, and anthracene.

In the odd minutes while he waited for mixtures to cool, he studied the English language. If he were to stay in England, he must be able to speak English fluently.

For six long, lonely weeks, his rigid schedule was brightened only by letters from Vera. His experiments led to a discovery which later proved valuable in cancer research.

Just as his funds were running low, a Manchester manufacturer asked Weizmann to do some chemical experiments. The pay was to be only three pounds a week, about fifteen dollars, but it would help.

Then Professor Perkin invited him to give a weekly lecture to the chemistry students at Victoria University. "You may speak on any branch of chemistry that you choose," he said.

Weizmann smiled broadly until he remembered his language problem. "How can I lecture in English?" he asked. "I can hardly make myself understood at the green-grocer's."

"You must, you must, Weizmann," Perkin urged. "You don't have to start until after the Christmas holiday.

Dr. Weizmann (second from left, first row) and some of the staff of Victoria University in 1912

With time to prepare, you will do well. I am counting on you."

Chaim Weizmann finally agreed to try. While the students and faculty were enjoying their holiday, Chaim labored over his lecture. He wrote out his first lecture word by word, consulting a dictionary for spelling and meaning and searching for the most fitting phrases.

When the university reopened, the chemistry students gathered in the lecture hall and watched the Russian-born lecturer enter. In his turn, Weizmann looked over his audience. The English students seemed so boisterous and carefree compared to the students he had known in Berlin and Geneva.

Weizmann arranged his papers on the lectern, raised his eyes to the class, and began. "I am a foreigner," he said. "I have been in this country only a few months. I am at your mercy. I will do my best, but I am sure to make mistakes. You may make all the jokes you want —after the lecture." Then he gave his prepared talk as the students listened politely.

As the days and weeks went by, lecturing became easier for Weizmann. Often students stayed after class to ask questions. Gradually Weizmann realized that these English students were just as devoted to their studies as those on the Continent.

Weizmann enjoyed the academic world so much that he could have stayed isolated in it for the rest of his life. Yet something inside him continued to nag.

One day a letter arrived from a friend in Pinsk, describing the continued tsarist persecution of the Jews. The letter rekindled his interest in helping his people obtain a land of their own.

That summer Weizmann attended the Zionist Congress in Vienna, the first scheduled meeting since Herzl died. The Zionists missed their founder's presence and his leadership, but they debated the Uganda offer once more. This time the Congress voted it down decisively. Their goal continued to be the establishment of a homeland in Palestine.

When Chaim Weizmann returned to Manchester, he began attending meetings of the local Zionist Society. He was disappointed because the programs had little substance. One night he listened to a speaker describe his boat trip across the English Channel; toward the end, the speaker casually mentioned visiting a synagogue in Brussels.

Chaim Weizmann believed that Zionist meetings should be devoted to Zionist subjects. He might not have expressed his opinion, but the chairman called on him. "Dr. Weizmann," he asked, "won't you offer a word of thanks to our speaker?"

Weizmann was too new to England and to its customs to know that he was expected to rise, compliment the speaker, and sit down. Instead, he stood up and declared, "This lecture had no intellectual content; it was beneath criticism."

As the members gasped at his audacity, Weizmann went on, "A Zionist society should discuss Zionist work. It should not waste its time on such trivia."

By the time he sat down, he had thoroughly shocked the Manchester Zionists. They avoided him for months afterward. Nevertheless, the Manchester Zionist Society took his criticism seriously enough to arrange more appropriate and meaningful lectures. The more challenging programs attracted the younger members, and soon Chaim Weizmann was invited to address the society. He became more involved, and gradually Manchester became the center of Zionist thought in England.

That winter, British Prime Minister Arthur Balfour was standing for election to Parliament from Liverpool. Balfour had heard of Chaim Weizmann and wanted to meet the young Russian–Jew who had led the opposition to the Uganda offer made by his government.

Dr. Weizmann went to the old-fashioned Queen's Hotel in Liverpool, where Balfour had his campaign headquarters. He was escorted through corridors jammed with people waiting to see the prime minister. As he was shown into Balfour's room, an aide told Weizmann, "Don't stay more than fifteen minutes. All these people want to see him too."

Balfour shook hands with the lecturer, then sat down, slumping into a chair, his long legs stretched out in front of him. The prime minister got to the heart of the matter immediately.

Balfour became a staunch supporter of Zionism and Chaim's life-long friend.

"Why do some Jews oppose the Uganda offer?" he asked. "The British government is truly anxious to relieve the misery of the Jews."

Chaim Weizmann cleared his throat, wishing that he had better command of the English language. "Only a deep religious conviction keeps this movement alive," he began. "This conviction is based on the establishment of a Jewish state in Palestine, and in Palestine alone. If Moses had come into the Zionist meeting when it was voting for Uganda, he would have broken the tablets again."

Weizmann looked at Balfour and began to perspire. Was Balfour's expression of courtesy only the mask of boredom? Chaim Weizmann was about to bow himself out of the room when Balfour started asking questions.

With his lightning perception, Weizmann sensed how much was turning on this conversation. "Mr. Balfour," he asked, "supposing I were to offer you Paris, instead of London. Would you take it?"

Balfour smiled, "But we have London."

"Yes," the lecturer said, "and we had Jerusalem when London was only a marsh."

"Are there many Jews who think as you do?" Balfour asked. "If so, where are they?"

Weizmann replied, "I speak for millions of Jews whom you may never see, and who cannot speak for themselves."

Balfour replied, "If that is so, you will one day be a force."

The interview was prolonged for one hour and a quarter. It was the beginning of a personal friendship and a chain of events far more important than either man foresaw.

7. The Newlyweds

Dr. Weizmann was soon making plans for the summer. Vera would graduate in June, and they agreed to have their wedding in Zoppot, Germany, a border town which at least Chaim's parents could reach.

On an August evening in 1906, the marriage canopy was set up in Zoppot's small synagogue. A fiddler played a traditional wedding song. Oser and Rachel Weizmann escorted their son to the canopy. Since Vera's family could not attend the wedding, Feivel and Miriam Weizmann, brother and sister of the professor, escorted the bride.

As Vera approached the canopy, the bridegroom reached for her hand. The rabbi read the time-honored words that made the couple man and wife. Chaim Weizmann placed a ring on Vera's finger; he crushed a wine glass under his heel in traditional remembrance of the destruction of the Temple in Jerusalem. Then, as Chaim bent to kiss his bride, the fiddler began playing a joyful tune. Although there were few people at the wedding, they sang and danced and rejoiced late into the evening.

The newlyweds went to Cologne for their honeymoon because Chaim wanted to attend a Zionist committee meeting there.

As they traveled by train, Vera teased, "The complete honeymoon should include a Zionist meeting."

They both laughed. "After the meeting, we will take a steamer trip on the Rhine," the bridegroom said. "There won't be any Zionist meetings on the steamer, and we'll be en route to England too."

In England, the newlyweds moved into the furnished rooms which Chaim had rented earlier. Manchester proved to be a lonely place for Vera. As she knew no English, she could not speak to anyone except her husband. Chaim tried to teach her English, but he was away all day, either lecturing or doing research. Many of his evenings and weekends were spent with Zionist groups. Vera stayed in their dreary rooms alone, reading, or she took long walks. She tried to teach herself English by reading the newspaper with the help of a dictionary. Gradually her use of the language improved.

Occasionally Vera visited her husband's laboratory, which she always found scrupulously clean. "Most laboratories have unused apparatus lying around," she commented, "but yours never does."

Chaim smiled. He had been granted several dyestuff patents and was now branching out into other areas. He had a patent for the production of synthetic camphor and was now doing research on proteins and amino acids.

Vera looked at the test tubes, which were labeled *bY*, *bc*, *AB*, and so on. "Are these protein cultures?" she asked.

"No," he said, "this is something different. I am trying to isolate a bacterium. If I can do it, it might mean a new breakthrough in chemistry. I think this bacterium can change starch into acetone and butyl alcohol."

"That seems a long way from your protein research," Vera said.

"I find that my research leads from one discovery to another," Chaim replied. "That's what I enjoy most about it. Of course, I have no use for the acetone, but I think the butyl alcohol can be converted into synthetic rubber."

Eventually Chaim did isolate the bacterium, and it was named after him: *Clostridium acetobutylicum Weizmann.*

That spring, the Weizmanns moved into a house with the low rental of 33 pounds a year, about $150. Even this amount strained their budget, for Chaim was continually sending money to help his younger brothers and sisters who were enrolled at various universities outside Russia. The Weizmanns, however, had decided they needed more than three rooms, for they were expecting a baby soon.

Vera was busy learning how to be a housewife in her new home, which she liked to call her "doll's house."

One day a butcher came to her door. "Would you like to buy some meat?" he asked.

"Yes," she replied. "We need meat."

The butcher fidgeted for a moment, waiting for her to name the cut. Vera, however, thought meat was meat. Finally, the butcher asked, "What cuts would you like?"

"Cuts?" Vera asked as she wrinkled her brow. "Yes, I suppose you must cut it."

The butcher realized that Mrs. Weizmann had no idea of what he meant. "Do you want a roast, a steak, or chops?" he asked.

"Do I have to choose?" Vera asked in amazement. "What's the difference?"

The butcher scratched his head. He had never met a housewife like Vera. He did not have time to explain every cut, so he gave her two steaks, took her money, and went on his way.

Vera knew that she had seemed stupid to the butcher. Now she had to do something with the steaks. She put them in a pot with water and boiled them for dinner.

"The butcher called these steaks," she said as she served her husband that night.

"Vera, Vera, I am not a cook, but I know that you're not supposed to boil steak," her husband said.

"Oh," moaned the young wife, "It's so frustrating to have a medical degree and not know the first thing about cooking."

Vera Weizmann

"You will learn," her husband said as he gallantly ate the boiled steak.

"Tomorrow I will buy a cookbook and study it," Vera said, and she kept her word.

The Weizmanns' first child, Benjamin, was born that summer. The baby cried frequently, and Vera stayed up night after night trying to soothe him.

Chaim noticed how pale and weary Vera looked. "I have an idea," he said. "We can take turns looking after the baby when he wakes up at night. I can work at the same time."

When Benjy cried, his father corrected papers while he bounced the baby up and down on his knee, and Vera was able to catch up on her sleep.

In the summer of 1907 Chaim Weizmann made a stirring speech at a Zionist Congress at the Hague.

After the speech, an industrialist asked him, "Why don't you go to Palestine?"

Weizmann answered honestly, "I can't afford the trip."

"Look, I will finance your trip," the industrialist said. "You are a chemist with practical experience. Go and see what industries can be established there."

So, instead of returning to his family in Manchester, Chaim Weizmann took a train to Marseille, France, and from there he took a ship to Palestine. He was excited as he stood at the rail, waiting for his first glimpse of the Holy Land.

The journey took longer than he anticipated. Finally someone yelled, "There it is! There's Jaffa."

Dr. Weizmann remembered that, according to the Bible, Jonah's ship had been wrecked within sight of Jaffa, and Jonah had been cast into this very sea and swallowed by a whale.

The ship docked, and Weizmann stepped onto the soil of the Holy Land. He saw streets full of Arabs in flowing white robes; he heard people speaking Arabic, a language that sounded a little like Hebrew. The sights and smells and sounds of a Middle Eastern city seemed strange to him.

Chaim Weizmann was glad to be in Palestine, yet he was also saddened as he traveled through the country, for he saw few patches of green and only a pitifully small number of straggly trees. Much of Palestine consisted of desert or swampland; even land that could be cultivated was barren and rocky. No wonder Dr. Weizmann had heard Palestine described as the most miserably neglected corner of the Turkish Empire!

At best the Turks were despotic rulers of Palestine, more interested in collecting taxes than in improving the country or the lives of its inhabitants.

The countryside was thinly populated by Arab *fellahin*, or tenant farmers, who did not own the land they worked. They struggled to raise crops and grazed their goats on the land, but these poverty-stricken fellahin did not have the resources to irrigate or improve the lands they farmed. They milked their goats and sometimes made cheeses. In order to earn enough money to pay rent to the wealthy *effendi* who were their landlords, they sold these cheeses and their spare animals and goatskins in the market. Often these effendi lived far away in Damascus or in other cities of the Middle East.

There were about 600,000 people living in Palestine, Dr. Weizmann estimated; most of them were Arabs, but 80,000 were Jews. Some of these Jews were descendants of those who had never left the Holy Land. A second group consisted of old, pious European Jews who had come here in their old age to die on holy soil.

Living mostly in such cities as Jerusalem, Safed, Haifa, and Hebron, these elderly Jews were supported by a system of charity collections in Europe; they spent their time studying sacred books. Dr. Weizmann knew these Jews were too old to help rebuild the Holy Land.

Another group of Jews had come from Russia within the past two decades and had established a thin line of agricultural colonies. Baron Edmond de Rothschild, a member of the international banking family, provided the funds to support them. Dr. Weizmann observed that these settlers acted as landowners and hired others to do the actual labor. While these colonies had persisted through heat, malaria, and Turkish persecutions, they were still dependent on Baron Rothschild's generosity.

Dr. Weizmann was far more pleased with the Zionist colonies he found in a few other places in Palestine. Here young men and women who had emigrated from Russia in the last few years were working the soil themselves. They were using their intelligence to restore the soil and raise their crops. Dr. Weizmann was also pleased to see that these Jews had established high schools.

During his travels in Palestine, Dr. Weizmann also visited the town of Rehovoth to see Aaron Eisenberg for whom he had collected kopecks so long ago in Pinsk. The two men embraced, and tears ran down their cheeks as they recalled their mutual friends.

Chaim Weizmann looked about him. "Rehovoth is

a lovely area," he said. "You have made trees grow here."

"Come," Eisenberg said, and he led his friend to an arid spot. "See how hard the soil is; the seasonal rains simply run off. But, see, with this spade I dig down, and what do we find? Fertile soil. That is the big task for us here: to find that fertile soil and to irrigate it. Some of us are developing cisterns and reservoirs to preserve the rain water. Others dig deep wells, and, if they are lucky, hit underground springs. Still others are working to pipe water from the rivers and irrigate the fields that way."

Dr. Weizmann visited Petach Tikvah (below), one of the earliest settlements founded by young Jews.

"I see," Weizmann said. "Someone has to take the time, and must love the land enough to make it fruitful."

"That is exactly what we Jews in these agricultural colonies are doing," Eisenberg said. "At least we are trying." He led his visitor back to his home. "On a clear day, you can see the mountains of Jerusalem from here."

"Someday," Chaim Weizmann said, "I would like to live here."

"Come back and stay," Eisenberg said as they bade each other farewell.

When Dr. Weizmann returned to his Manchester home, his wife greeted him affectionately, and then asked, "What was the best part of Palestine, Chaimchik?"

"The air," he told her. "The air is so pure, you can look back 3,000 years."

8. Wartime Chemist

Several happy, productive years in Manchester followed for the Weizmanns. Dr. Weizmann had gathered about him men who worked for Zionism, and their fellowship became known as the Manchester school of Zionism.

Vera passed the British medical exams and took a position as a medical officer, supervising seven clinics for babies and expectant mothers in Manchester's slum areas.

Benjy, healthy and growing, was an inquisitive child. "His questions show an insight into the world," his proud father claimed.

"Oh, Chaimchik," Vera protested. "All children ask questions."

"But not such intelligent ones," the father insisted.

As he became more at home with English, Weizmann found teaching easier. His chemical research brought him prestige as he published many scientific papers.

As a result of his ever-widening reputation as a chemist, he was awarded a Doctorate of Science degree by Victoria University.

Nevertheless, Dr. Weizmann felt there was more to learn about chemistry. So he spent his summer vacations at the Pasteur Institute in Paris, where he studied bacteriology. As he increased his own knowledge, he began offering classes in biochemistry to his students.

Then came the first break in the family circle. In 1912, a telegram brought the sad news that Oser Weizmann, exhausted from hard work, had died at the age of sixty.

In their sorrow, Chaim and Vera Weizmann found comfort in recalling Oser's remarkable achievement—nine of his twelve children were university graduates.

Shortly afterward, a professorship became vacant at the university. Dr. Weizmann confidently expected the appointment, but the chair went instead to a relative of Professor Perkin. This appointment surprised the entire staff.

Dr. Weizmann was angry and depressed; he felt it was not just. When a German university offered him a position, he was all set to take the new post. Vera, however, refused to go.

"Go," Vera said, "but you will go alone. I will not go to Germany."

"But you are so unreasonable," Dr. Weizmann argued. "In Germany I will receive proper recognition for my research."

"Let us see who is unreasonable," Vera said. "You have been telling me for years how the Germans hate the Jews, and how blind the German Jews are. You have also been telling me for years that the path to the Holy Land lies through England. Now, because your feelings are hurt, you want to go to Germany. I will not go."

In his pique, Dr. Weizmann did not speak to Vera for three weeks, but she did not give in. Dr. Weizmann gradually got over his disappointment.

It was not long before he was glad Vera had refused to move. In 1914, Germany invaded Belgium and France. England and Russia, allies of the invaded nations, went to their aid. Austria lined up with Germany. World War I had begun.

Dr. Weizmann feared for his mother when he heard that the Germans were attacking Pinsk. Rachel, widowed and sixty years old, had already endured many hardships. One day he received word that she had found sanctuary in Warsaw. But his relief was short-lived, for Germany soon invaded Warsaw. Then somehow Rachel managed to flee from the Germans to safety in Moscow.

Meanwhile the British War Office sent Dr. Weizmann and all scientists an invitation to share any discovery of military importance with the government. Dr. Weizmann promptly wrote the War Office about his research on acetone, a clear inflammable liquid used in the manufacture of explosives.

There was no immediate reply, so he continued his academic routine. One of his former students, waiting to be called by the army, visited his teacher. He found Dr. Weizmann in a dark corner of his laboratory, bending over a test tube. The older man's somewhat awesome appearance quickly changed as he paused and looked up with a smile of greeting.

"I am free to help you if I can be of any use," the younger man said.

Dr. Weizmann's smile widened. "You are just what I need, someone to take over, develop, and evaluate the cultures."

"I'm glad to help, but remember, I don't know too much about your work."

"You will do excellent work," Dr. Weizmann assured him and gave him a job right away.

A few weeks later, Dr. Weizmann took a bunch of keys from his chain and handed them to his assistant as he announced, "I am going to London." He was cheerful and excited. "You will run this laboratory."

His assistant gasped, "When are you coming back?"

"The British Admiralty has summoned me," Dr. Weizmann said. "That's all I know."

Dr. Weizmann packed a small bag, kissed his wife and son good-bye, and left on the next train. In London, he met the first lord of the admiralty, Winston Churchill.

Churchill, appointed to the post in 1911, had warned his countrymen that Germany would start a war. When World War I broke out, the British navy, thanks to Churchill, was prepared, but the army was not.

Churchill wasted no words. "Well, Dr. Weizmann," he said. "We need 30,000 tons of acetone to keep our naval guns supplied. Can you make it?"

Dr. Weizmann gulped. Somehow he managed to answer, "I am only a research chemist. I know how to produce acetone in small quantities. So far I have succeeded in making only a few hundred cubic centimeters of acetone at a time."

"If you can make a small amount, just multiply and make a larger amount," Churchill suggested briskly.

"It is mostly a question of brewing," Dr. Weizmann explained. "I'll need big vats, the kind gin distilleries have, for the amount you want."

"Fine, fine, we'll get you a distillery," Churchill agreed.

"But I will also need assistants and equipment and supplies," Dr. Weizmann said.

"You shall have whatever you need, Dr. Weizmann," Churchill said.

Dr. Weizmann inspected one distillery after another to find one suitable for developing the production of acetone. Finally he found a plant he could use, but the owner was unhappy. "I don't want my plant converted to war production," he grumbled. "I'll be losing thousands of pounds in profits and all my customers."

Dr. Weizmann replied, "If England does not win this war, you will never again make any money."

The unhappy owner finally agreed, and Dr. Weizmann

moved his assistants and his chemical supplies into the distillery.

Time was most important, for the navy's supply of acetone was shrinking daily. To get production going as rapidly as possible, Dr. Weizmann decided to use the distillery vats without sterilizing them first. He and his assistants began making the acetone by running water into the vats, shaking in corn by hand, and gradually raising the temperature to a boil; they were trying to make the corn mash sterile. Then it was cooled and innoculated with the bacterium. But the first fermentation ended in failure.

Dr. Weizmann went over each step of the process. "I think we must start all over again and sterilize these vats. We tried to save time and, instead, we wasted it."

This time Dr. Weizmann and his assistants washed and sterilized every piece of equipment, including the large vats. Even then, with the navy's supply of acetone running low, Dr. Weizmann did not know if he could succeed.

Once again the corn was put in the vats, boiled, cooled, and innoculated with the bacterium. Now Weizmann could only wait. The fermentation would require from 9 A.M. one day until 3 P.M. the following day. Dr. Weizmann had long since learned the art of sleeping for short stretches in noisy and uncomfortable places. He sent his assistants home. "You'd better get some sleep," he told them.

"But what about you, Dr. Weizmann?" they asked. "I'll stay at the distillery," he said. "I'll rest after we succeed."

The hours crept by like a sleepy snail. All night long Dr. Weizmann checked the temperature, the equipment, and the formula at regular intervals.

Finally 3 P.M. arrived. His assistants were there as Dr. Weizmann went to the door of the first vat. Everyone held his breath as Dr. Weizmann opened the door. The fruity odor struck their nostrils, and they saw the colorless liquid. They knew the process was a success! The vats were filled with 500 gallons of acetone.

How Dr. Weizmann and his assistants laughed! They put their arms around one another and did an impromptu dance. They knew that their success meant acetone could be produced in large quantities, and the navy's guns could continue to defend England.

The war was grim, however. A great naval battle with heavy English losses took place near Gallipoli, Turkey. Turkey had entered the war on the German side. Winston Churchill, criticized bitterly for this defeat, resigned his admiralty post and joined the army in France as a lieutenant colonel. Arthur James Balfour, the statesman Dr. Weizmann had met years before, took Churchill's place as first lord of the admiralty.

Since Dr. Weizmann's work was centered in London, he and Vera bought a home there early in 1916. Here their second son, Michael, was born in November 1916.

The following month Churchill was recalled to London to serve as minister of munitions. He summoned Dr. Weizmann to his office. Bluntly, Churchill declared, "We need more acetone, much more."

"We're producing all we can in this distillery," Dr. Weizmann said.

"Then get other distilleries," Churchill barked.

Once again Dr. Weizmann inspected distilleries. He sought out former students and talked them into helping him. He trained young chemists in his procedures at the London distillery; then he sent them to take charge of distilleries throughout England, Scotland, and Ireland.

Just as production seemed to be running smoothly, Dr. Weizmann hit another snag. The British farmers were growing all the corn they possibly could, but without larger quantities, sufficient acetone could not be produced.

The United States had plenty of corn and was trying to ship it to England, but German submarines were sinking the ships.

Dr. Weizmann experimented with other grains. Wheat proved just as effective, but was equally scarce. He tried horse chestnuts, and these worked too. He enlisted classes of school children to scour the countryside for nuts. Even Queen Mary joined in this effort, but there were not enough horse chestnuts for large-scale production of acetone.

In April 1917, the United States entered the war. The

American and British governments decided to produce acetone in the United States and in Canada where there was an abundant supply of grain.

Now that the production of acetone was moving ahead smoothly, Dr. Weizmann turned toward other scientific problems. His work continued to bring him in contact with a great many British statesmen, and gave him the opportunity to present his views on Palestine to some of the most influential men of his day.

The Weizmann home became a gathering place for Zionists and for those whom Weizmann had interested in the Zionist cause.

In March 1917, news of the Russian Revolution had reached England. By April, Lenin and his lieutenants in the radical wing of the revolutionary party—called Bolsheviks—were back in Russia, and struggling with more moderate groups for control of the government.

The Jewish population had been treated ruthlessly by both the Russian and German armies, which had swept back and forth across the Pale. Now, added to their misery, was the fear of what the revolution might bring. To Dr. Weizmann it seemed more urgent than ever to press for the establishment of a Jewish homeland.

At a meeting with Balfour, Dr. Weizmann expressed his feelings to the first lord of the admiralty.

"You know," Balfour replied, "I often remember that first conversation of ours. I believe that when the guns stop firing, you may get Jerusalem."

9. The Balfour Declaration

Dr. Weizmann was delighted that Balfour and other British statesmen were sympathetic to the idea of a Jewish national home. These men, such as Churchill and David Lloyd George, had been nurtured on Bible history in childhood and understood the age-old longings of the Jews for a return to Palestine.

The British army was at this time fighting Turkish and German forces in the Middle East in order to prevent the Suez Canal from falling into enemy hands. Dr. Weizmann knew that if the British should succeed in driving the Turks out of Palestine and neighboring states, they would themselves become a force in the Middle East. British leaders would then be in a position to help in the establishment of a Jewish homeland in Palestine.

The Jewish population in Palestine had increased to 100,000 in the years following Dr. Weizmann's first visit. Many still lived in cities, but now more and more of the young settlers tilled the soil in some fifty thriving agricultural communities.

Most of these Jews felt their future lay with the democratic nations of the West. With the Turks supporting the Germans, the Palestinian Jews worked secretly for the British. They reported that a German commander was in Palestine to marshal German and Turkish troops for an attack on the Suez Canal. Such a plan, if successful, would cut Great Britain's lifeline to its Far East empire.

When the Turks learned that the Jews were aiding the British, they arrested Jews indiscriminately and sent hundreds of them to special camps and prisons. Others were hanged. Fearful for their lives, many others fled to British-held Egypt. By 1917, the Jewish population had been cut in half, and much of the hard work of the early settlers was destroyed.

In the autumn of 1917, the British war cabinet, confident of winning the war, held long deliberations about Jewish claims to Palestine. The British leaders frequently consulted Dr. Weizmann.

Balfour, however, was the minister who devoted the most time to the subject. In his most persuasive tones, he urged the cabinet, "When the war is over, let's give the Zionists an opportunity to try out their great experiment."

Before presenting the formal motion supporting a Jewish homeland in Palestine, Balfour rewrote it twelve times. Most people felt that the motion would have little trouble gaining a majority of votes.

David Lloyd George (left) and Winston Churchill (right) supported the idea of a Jewish national home.

However, Dr. Weizmann, now president of the English Zionist Federation, learned that opposition was coming from another Jew, Sir Edwin Montagu. Sir Edwin had been brought up in England and consequently did not understand how much the Jews of Russia, Poland, and Rumania had suffered from pogroms. As a prosperous citizen of a free nation, he saw no need for a Jewish state.

Montagu said, "Since Jews are a religious community, and nothing more, the utmost that can be demanded

87

for the Jews of Palestine is enjoyment of religious and civil liberty, reasonable facilities for immigration and colonization, and municipal privileges."

"Montagu reminds me," Dr. Weizmann told Vera, "of the Pfungstadt headmaster." He saw that Montagu could ruin the Zionist dream of self-rule. At the same time, Dr. Weizmann hoped that Herbert Samuel, another Jew in the British government, and a Zionist, could offset Montagu's arguments.

Samuel was helpful, but as a result of the opposition of Montagu and some other British Jews, the original wording of Balfour's declaration was changed. Instead of recommending that Palestine become "the National Home of the Jewish people," it called for "the Establishment *in* Palestine of *a* National Home for the Jewish people." The wording was too vague, Weizmann thought ruefully. It could mean just about anything. Still, he decided, even this declaration was better than nothing.

Discussions in the British war cabinet went on interminably, it seemed to Dr. Weizmann. Finally November 2 was named as the day when the British cabinet would vote on the Palestine declaration in its final form.

As the cabinet members began filing into the War Office, Dr. Weizmann stood outside in the corridor and greeted each man. He smiled at Balfour and Samuel; he exchanged a few words with Churchill and nodded politely to Montagu.

Then Dr. Weizmann stepped over to a secretary and

asked, "Suppose the cabinet wanted me to answer some questions. Wouldn't it be a good idea for me to stay here and be available?"

"Dr. Weizmann," the secretary said sympathetically, "ever since the British government began, nobody other than an elected member has ever been admitted to a cabinet session. Go back to your laboratory; everything will be all right."

Dr. Weizmann was too restless to return to the calm of his laboratory. He wanted to stay near the War Office, so he entered a nearby room to wait out the meeting.

Meanwhile the members of the British cabinet had one last discussion before voting. Montagu stood up and declared, "The Jews do not need a homeland. If some Jews want to go to Palestine and live privately, that is all right, but they do not need a nation of their own."

Then Arthur Balfour suggested, "Let's ask Dr. Weizmann to state his position."

The cabinet dispatched a messenger to summon Dr. Weizmann. The messenger, however, could not find him anywhere. He reported to the cabinet that Dr. Weizmann was not in his laboratory, and not at home.

"I have known Dr. Weizmann for many years," Balfour said. "I think I can present his arguments." And he did.

Finally the cabinet voted. The Balfour Declaration received a majority of the votes. It read:

> His Majesty's government views with favor the establishment in Palestine of a National Home for the Jewish people, and will use their best endeavors to facilitate the achievement of this object, it being clearly understood that nothing shall be done which may prejudice the civil and religious rights of the existing non-Jewish communities in Palestine or the rights and political status enjoyed by Jews in any other country.

When the meeting was over, Dr. Weizmann was waiting in the corridor. The British statesmen crowded around him to shake hands and to congratulate him. Dr. Weizmann was sorry that the declaration voted on was so much weaker than the original version. Still he was overjoyed that the historic statement of policy had finally been passed.

When Dr. Weizmann reached his home, he found Zionist friends and government supporters crowding the rooms; everyone looked positively light-headed with joy. The Balfour Declaration marked the first time in nearly 2,000 years that a world power had officially recognized the right of Jews to a national home in the Holy Land.

The following days were crammed with receptions and meetings. Dr. Weizmann accompanied Balfour on a triumphal tour through London's East End. The poor Jews who lived in the area—many of them immigrants from eastern Europe—filled the streets in a delirious demonstration of gratitude.

Dr. Weizmann told Balfour, "These are the Jews you never see; the streets of Pinsk are paved with them."

The French and Italian governments supported the Balfour Declaration. The American President Woodrow Wilson cabled, "In Palestine shall be laid the foundations of a Jewish commonwealth."

Although Dr. Weizmann rejoiced with other Jews in the passage of the Balfour Declaration, he knew that the hard work was just beginning. The Zionists had to transform their ideals into reality.

Dr. Weizmann took the first step in this direction by heading, at the request of the British, the Zionist Commission, composed of representatives of Jews from most of the Allied nations. The commission planned to visit Palestine early in 1918, even before the Holy Land was completely freed from the Turks. Its purpose was to make recommendations "in the spirit of the Balfour Declaration."

In March 1918, the commission set sail.

10. Palestine in Wartime

When Dr. Weizmann and the other members of the Zionist Commission reached Palestine, there was danger all around. The Turkish and Allied forces were still fighting each other. While the Allies held some of Palestine, the Turkish forces were only two miles from the city of Jerusalem.

Dr. Weizmann and his companions traveled through those areas of the Holy Land that were held by the Allies. They knew that three different groups of people must be considered in putting the Balfour Declaration to work. There were the Arabs, the Jews, and the British military who would soon be in control of the country.

The British military thought Dr. Weizmann and all Zionists were mad to want such a wasteland for their people. The officers said, "Palestine is a land of sand and heat, mosquitoes and malaria, rocks and swamps. You can see for yourself. We can hardly wait to leave."

"Ah, but the Jews will fertilize the soil and water it," Dr. Weizmann told them. "They will fulfill the biblical prophecy and make the desert bloom. The Balfour

Declaration states that this will be a Jewish national home."

"The Balfour Declaration?" one officer asked. "What's that? We never heard of it."

Dr. Weizmann explained the paper issued by the officers' own government, but the men shrugged their shoulders. They listened politely, but they did not believe anyone could make the rocky sand of Palestine bloom. Many of them were, in any case, hostile to the aspirations of the Jews.

Dr. Weizmann wanted to discuss the Balfour Declaration with Emir Feisal, commander-in-chief of the Arab army. Although the Turks ruled the lands of the Middle East, an Arab army led by Feisal was fighting on the side of the British. In 1916, Feisal's father had been persuaded to support the Allied cause in exchange for a British promise to establish three Arab kingdoms in the Mideast after the war. These kingdoms would be under the control of Feisal and his two brothers.

Now Emir Feisal led 10,000 Arabs, who felt that they were fighting for their independence. Dr. Weizmann thought that a discussion with Feisal was essential to the future development of Palestine.

Before he could visit Emir Feisal, however, Dr. Weizmann had an unexpected caller. The visitor was Corporal David Ben Gurion, a brash young soldier from the Jewish Legion. This was the group of Palestinian volunteers who were fighting against Turkey under

British command. The Jewish Legion was the first all-Jewish military unit since the time of the Roman conquest of the Holy Land. Ben Gurion had come from Russia to live in Palestine three years before at the age of eighteen. Already he was known both as a journalist and as a leader among the young Jewish settlers.

Dr. Weizmann shook hands with Ben Gurion and answered the young man's questions. The famed scientist patiently explained what the Balfour Declaration meant politically for the Palestinian Jews.

As he was about to leave, the corporal confessed that he was absent from the Jewish legion without permission. "I had to hear about the Balfour Declaration from you," he said.

Dr. Weizmann starts on the first leg of his roundabout journey to visit Emir Feisal.

The next day Dr. Weizmann set out with a British aide to visit Emir Feisal in Transjordan, then a part of Palestine. Because the Turks still held the Jordan Valley, Dr. Weizmann had to take a roundabout route. He traveled by train to Suez, then by ship for six days to Aqaba, and then finally north through the burning desert by car. The last part of the exhausting journey was on foot.

Arabs on camelback came to greet him, bearing gifts of water and bread, traditional offerings of hospitality. They also brought Emir Feisal's welcome.

Weary from the long trip and the oppressive heat, Dr. Weizmann decided to postpone his audience with Emir Feisal until the following day; then he would be more rested. That evening he took a walk in the bright moonlight. As he looked down upon the Jordan Valley and the Dead Sea and to the Judean hills beyond, Dr. Weizmann felt a little like Moses in this land which God had promised to his people.

The next morning he was escorted to Emir Feisal's tent where the Arab leader was waiting to receive him. Emir Feisal looked very tall and slender in his long white robes; he wore a brown headcloth bound with a brilliant scarlet and gold cord. He was surrounded by warriors. Colonel T.E. Lawrence, an officer in the British army, was there too. Lawrence had helped organize the Arab revolt against the Turks and had helped draw Feisal into the war on the British side.

After greeting Dr. Weizmann, Emir Feisal lifted his hand signaling a servant to bring a breakfast tray. The meal consisted of dates, biscuits, cereals, and small cups of tea.

When they had finished eating, everyone withdrew, leaving Dr. Weizmann and Emir Feisal alone. Only Lawrence remained to act as an interpreter in the discussions.

"Let us remember that the Jews and the Arabs are cousins," Dr. Weizmann said as he explained the Zionist mission.

"There is room here for your people and mine in the Middle East," Emir Feisal responded warmly. "Let us continue our tradition of friendship."

"I have a vision," Dr. Weizmann said, "of an Arab culture and a Jewish culture flowering side by side."

"The Jews can be of help to the Arabs," Lawrence said. "The Jews will bring their scientific knowledge and make the land productive. Certainly the Arab world stands to gain much from a Jewish homeland in Palestine."

Before Dr. Weizmann left, the emir suggested they be photographed together. "Let us always remain friends as we are in this picture," he said graciously.

Encouraged by Emir Feisal's friendliness and by Lawrence's support, Chaim Weizmann returned to Jerusalem. It was almost time to go back to England, but there was one more thing he wanted to do. Plans for the Hebrew University had been shelved because of the war; Dr. Weizmann wanted to revive those plans.

"I want to lay the cornerstone for the Hebrew University," he told General Edmund Allenby, the British military commander. "I want to do it before I leave."

"University!" General Allenby scoffed. "Remember, Dr. Weizmann, the Turks are battling us only two miles from Jerusalem."

"I refuse to be discouraged," Dr. Weizmann replied. "I can't predict when the university will actually be built. I certainly don't know how it will be paid for, but I will lay the cornerstone as my act of faith."

This historic photograph of Dr. Weizmann and Emir Feisal was taken as a memento of their meeting.

The British military leaders were positive that Dr. Weizmann was either a madman or, from the fervor in his eye, a prophet.

The commander said, "You have chosen the worst possible time, but you seem determined. Go ahead; break ground for your university."

The groundbreaking ceremony was scheduled for an afternoon in July 1918. The sun flooded the hills with a golden light as leaders of the Moslem, Christian, and Jewish religious communities of Jerusalem gathered on Mount Scopus.

Dr. Weizmann dug up the first shovelful of earth to break the ground, and one symbolic stone was laid. Then Dr. Weizmann spoke to the assemblage: "In the darkest ages of our existence, we Jews found protection and shelter within the walls of our schools and colleges, and in the devoted study of Jewish science, the tormented Jew found relief and consolation."

Dr. Weizmann ended his speech by stating, "This dedication in the midst of war shows the Jewish people's determination to go beyond our own restoration, and to make a contribution to humanity. This is an act of faith. Time alone will prove if our faith is justified."

The entire ceremony lasted less than an hour. When it was over, everyone sang "Hatikvah" and "God Save the King." No one seemed anxious to leave, and the group stood silent with bowed heads around the cornerstone while the twilight deepened.

11. Years of Travel

By late autumn, Dr. Weizmann was back in London. He hugged Benjy, who was growing taller, and tossed little Michael in the air. Then he turned to Vera and embraced her. Later he would read the accumulated mail and catch up on the work that waited for his attention.

Dr. Weizmann had made a date to have lunch with Prime Minister David Lloyd George on November 11, 1918, and to report on his trip. That morning he was putting his notes together, and Vera was brushing his jacket, when a messenger arrived.

Dr. Weizmann took the envelope and opened it.

"What is it?" Vera asked. Her husband was too overwhelmed to speak. He swallowed hard, then managed to say, "The war is over; the Germans have given up, and an armistice has been declared."

"How wonderful!" said Vera, tears springing to her eyes. "Maybe now we will hear from our families again."

"Perhaps the prime minister will want to cancel our engagement," Dr. Weizmann said. He telephoned and was told to come as planned.

There were so many people out in the streets, rejoicing at the news, that Dr. Weizmann's taxi proceeded slowly. When he reached 10 Downing Street, hundreds of people were crowded outside the prime minister's residence.

Dr. Weizmann paid the taxicab driver, wove through the crowd to reach the door, and showed the constable on duty his calling card.

Dr. Weizmann was ushered into the prime minister's office. The British leader was sitting by the window reading the Psalms. He was so moved by the ending of the terrible war that there were tears in his eyes as he greeted Dr. Weizmann.

"We have just sent off seven trains full of bread and other essential food to be distributed in Germany," the prime minister said.

The two men talked a few minutes and then Lloyd George told Dr. Weizmann, "You helped the Allied nations win this war with your new method of making acetone. Now, with your work in Palestine, you are changing the map of the world."

"The British surely are the ones who have changed the map of the world," Dr. Weizmann gallantly responded.

At last the two men settled down to lunch, and Dr. Weizmann had an opportunity to report on events in Palestine.

Shortly afterward, Dr. Weizmann was able to sell his

acetone patents to an American firm. This assured him of a comfortable income for some time to come.

With the war effort behind him, Dr. Weizmann began studying the effects of the war on the Jewish people. The Jews in eastern Europe had suffered bitterly at the hands of both the Russian and the German armies. The German Jews who had supported their government were impoverished. The Russian Jews were caught up in the civil war which was devastating their land.

The Jews of the Russian Pale, who had been the mainstay of the Zionist movement, were no longer able to help in the practical work of building a Jewish homeland. This task, therefore, would have to be assumed by the Jews of western Europe and the United States.

In the autumn of 1919, Dr. Weizmann journeyed to Palestine. This time his wife went with him.

"It's about time," Vera said, "that I saw the land that has dominated my life for so long."

When the Weizmanns arrived in Palestine, the country was arid; the trees were gray with dust. There had been no rain for five months.

In their travels Vera noticed some Jewish pioneer women working on the roads; they were breaking rocks and stones with sledgehammers. Vera made it her business to speak to these hardworking women. She found that they were working as much as ten to twelve hours a day on a poor diet. Other pioneer women carried heavy loads and worked in the fields side by side with the men.

Jewish pioneer women herded sheep, tilled the soil, and labored at heavy tasks in the early settlements.

Vera resolved to interest her British friends in the plight of these laboring women and to raise funds to help them.

Dr. Weizmann, meanwhile, was busy finding homes and jobs for Jews returning to the Holy Land after the war. Among these were young people from the broken Jewish communities of Poland and other countries in central and eastern Europe. In some instances Dr. Weizmann found their trek had lasted for months and had carried them from the Ukraine to Japan and back across India and Persia. Some came with a rudimentary training in agriculture; most, however, brought only their bare hands and their devotion.

"These are fine people," Dr. Weizmann commented to Vera. "We must make plans for their reception. We must have a budget to help them get started. We have a tremendous undertaking here. It will be up to world Jewry to help these pioneers financially."

When Dr. and Mrs. Weizmann returned to London, they learned that Emir Feisal had sent a heartwarming letter to the World Zionist Organization. The letter reaffirmed the hopes of Dr. Weizmann and the emir. It read:

> We feel that the Arabs and Jews are cousins in race, suffering similar oppressions at the hands of powers stronger than themselves, and by a happy coincidence have been able to take the first step toward the attainment of their national ideals together.
>
> We Arabs, especially the educated among us, look with the deepest sympathy on the Zionist movement. . . . We will wish the Jews a most hearty welcome home. . . .
>
> With the chiefs of your movement, especially with Dr. Weizmann, we have had, and continue to have, the closest relations. He has been a great helper of our cause, and I hope the Arabs may soon

be in a position to make the Jews some return for their kindness. We are working together for a reformed and revived Near East and our two movements complete one another. The Jewish movement is national and not imperialistic. Our movement is national and not imperialistic, and there is room . . . for us both. Indeed, I think that neither can be a real success without the other. . . .

I look forward, and my people with me look forward, to a future in which we will help you and you will help us, so that the countries in which we are mutually interested may once again take their place in the community of civilized peoples of the world.

Yours sincerely,
Feisal

"What a remarkable letter," Dr. Weizmann commented upon reading it. "It should interest those who accuse us of beginning our Zionist work in Palestine without consulting the wishes of the Arabs."

Soon afterward, Dr. Weizmann received word that his mother, Rachel, had escaped Russia with her son Feivel and his family. They were going to Palestine.

Dr. Weizmann sent them funds to help them buy a home in Haifa overlooking the bay.

When he heard that they were settled, Dr. Weizmann decided to spend the Passover of 1920 with them.

"Benjy," he said to his twelve-year-old son, "you're almost a man. It's about time you saw the Holy Land."

So the father and son set out on the journey. Dr. Weizmann enjoyed having Benjy with him.

They spent a few days in Jerusalem. There Dr. Weizmann became alarmed when he heard his Arab friends speaking about one Haj Amin el Husseini, a member of a powerful Arab family in Palestine. Haj Amin, like other effendi, was troubled because wherever a Jewish settlement sprang up—green, tidy, and productive—the fellahin became dissatisfied. These fellahin lived in villages full of disease, where food was scarce and shelter primitive; they worked as hard as the Jews did, but they had nothing left after they paid their rent.

Some fellahin went to work for wages in the Jewish vineyards and groves instead of laboring hopelessly as semiserfs in eternal debt to the effendi. Some of them were seeking higher wages from their Arab employers and charging more money for the cheeses and goatskins which they sold in the market. It became apparent to Haj Amin and to other effendi that, if they wanted their comfortable way of life to continue, they would have to arouse the fellahin against the Jews.

Some of the younger Arabs were also hostile to Jewish immigration. Many of them were becoming fervent patriots as they responded to the independence movements of surrounding Arab countries; they loved Palestine and wanted to bind the country to Arab tradition. These young nationalists were convinced by extremists that Jewish settlement blocked their aims.

Haj Amin welded together followers from among all these groups and soon became a powerful political leader in Palestine.

He felt that it would be easy to stir up trouble and to turn all classes of Arabs against the Jews. The easiest way to arouse passion, he knew, was on a religious issue. Consequently he spread rumors of a Jewish plot to seize the Mosque of Omar, the Moslems' holy shrine in Jerusalem.

Dr. Weizmann told the British military commander in Jerusalem that he feared trouble. "I have had some experience with the atmosphere that precedes pogroms; I can feel the tensions here," he said.

"The town is full of troops," the commander said. "There can't be any trouble."

"Your troops will be useless because the attack will be over before the troops can reach the action," Dr. Weizmann said.

"Go ahead and enjoy your Passover," the commander said. "Don't worry."

Against his better judgment, Dr. Weizmann went on

to Haifa with Benjy, arriving there on Passover Eve. There was great joy as Rachel greeted her son and hugged her grandson.

"Since I was a child," Rachel said, "we kept repeating 'next year in Jerusalem' at every Passover seder. This year we will have our seder in the Holy Land."

"And Jerusalem is not far away," Benjy added.

"Come, sit down," Rachel urged. "It's time to begin."

Chaim Weizmann, his son, his brother Feivel, Feivel's family, and Grandmother Rachel sat down at the festive holiday table and read together the ancient story of Moses leading their ancestors out of slavery in Egypt to freedom. This was the story the Jews repeated every Passover. For the Weizmanns gathered in Haifa, the history, known almost by heart, had added meaning.

Meanwhile in Jerusalem, Haj Amin told Arabs assembled at the Mosque of Omar that the Jews were plotting to seize the mosque. The Arabs, now aroused and angry, marched through the streets, attacking any Jews they happened to meet.

The Jews, caught unaware, offered practically no resistance, Dr. Weizmann learned later. Jewish shops were looted; two Jewish girls were attacked, and four Jews were killed.

By the time Dr. Weizmann arrived in Jerusalem, quiet reigned in the city. Benjy, who was with him, asked, "How can a pogrom happen here? Who is guilty? Will they be punished?"

Dr. Weizmann did not know how to answer his son, for right after the pogrom, Haj Amin had fled from Jerusalem to safety in Syria, a neighboring Arab state. Although the British had in his absence tried and sentenced him to fifteen years in prison, he remained free in Syria.

To help regain his own peace of mind, Dr. Weizmann took a walk into the hills to be by himself for a little while, and to look toward the hills "whence cometh strength."

Soon it was time to leave Palestine and take Benjy back to London. In London Dr. Weizmann repacked his bags and left for San Remo, Italy, where representatives of the victorious Allied nations were gathering to decide many questions. One was the future of Palestine.

The decision on Palestine was put off until the last few hours of the conference. Dr. Weizmann nervously paced the hall, waiting for the delegates to emerge from the council chamber.

At long last the men came out and congratulated Dr. Weizmann on his successful work for the Zionist cause. The Allies had confirmed the Balfour Declaration and had drawn up a set of rules by which it would be carried out. England was given a mandate to govern Palestine and to assist in the establishment of a Jewish national home there.

That evening, Dr. Weizmann and representatives

of the Arabs dined together in celebration of the hopeful turn of events.

When Dr. Weizmann returned to London, he was pleased to learn that Sir Herbert Samuel, one of the men in the British wartime cabinet which had adopted the Balfour Declaration, had been named high commissioner of Palestine.

That summer, Dr. Weizmann also learned, the Zionist Congress was scheduled to meet for the first time since the war.

At the Congress, Chaim Weizmann attracted special attention. The role he had played in obtaining the Balfour Declaration was known to everyone.

When Dr. Weizmann rose to speak, his words were measured, his phrases incisive. He spoke of difficulties and of opportunities.

"The Balfour Declaration and the San Remo decision are the beginning of a new era for the Zionist dream of self-rule in a Jewish National Home in Palestine," he declared.

Chaim Weizmann was accepted as the leader of the new era. When elections were held at the end of the Congress, Dr. Weizmann became president of the World Zionist Organization. He drank deep of the joyousness of the occasion, but he did not forget the work that waited to be done.

In his closing speech, Dr. Weizmann stated that "a country which has lain waste for centuries, a country ... desolate and disease-ridden, cannot be transformed into a Jewish homeland by a declaration. Only action can bring about the fulfillment of the dream; and this action must be prompt."

"In Palestine," he declared, "nothing is ready. Everything is yet to be done, and we are at present building a country from the very rock. I trust to God that a Jewish state will come about; but it will not come about through political declarations, but by the sweat and blood of the Jewish people. That is the only way to build up a state."

Dr. Weizmann paused for a moment, then added, "If there is to be a Jewish state in the future, it depends largely upon us. We have it in our hands to make a truth, to make a reality of Palestine. When the history of this time is written, let our children in reading it see that their fathers did not waste their time, or their opportunity."

12. The First American Visit

The following spring of 1921, Chaim and Vera Weizmann sailed from Southampton for New York. Dr. Weizmann wanted to enlist the support of American Jews for the Jewish national home; he was seeking contributions for the Hebrew University and for the Jewish National Fund which provided money for reforestation and agricultural projects in Palestine. The Jewish National Fund had been initiated by one of the early Zionist Congresses.

Their ship arrived in New York harbor about noon on Saturday, April 2. Since it was the Sabbath, the Weizmanns decided to wait for sundown before they went ashore. Then they planned to go straight to their hotel to rest.

Their plans, however, had to be changed. Long before sundown, thousands of pious Jews, who would not ride on the Sabbath, had walked long distances from Brooklyn and the Bronx to welcome Chaim Weizmann, architect of the Balfour Declaration.

Other delegations arrived in cars, all of them decorated with the Jewish flag. Every car blew its horn.

By the time the Weizmanns got off the ship and went through customs, the people crowding the dock created a pandemonium.

The car, which the Weizmanns thought would take them quickly and quietly to their hotel, fell in at the end of a long procession, which led them through the lower East Side of New York where many Jewish immigrants lived. Their driver proceeded at a snail's pace while Chaim and Vera waved to the cheering Jews who jammed the sidewalks.

It was 11:30 P.M. before the Weizmanns reached their hotel. Tired, hungry, thirsty, and dazed, they walked into the hotel lobby to find another enthusiastic, cheering throng. They smiled as they listened to several speeches of welcome.

"Thank you, thank you," Dr. Weizmann said, and spoke briefly. It was long after midnight before the Weizmanns were alone in their room and could rest.

The next day the largest Jewish mass demonstration ever seen in New York greeted Dr. Weizmann at the Armory. There he was formally welcomed by a national Jewish committee.

"You are Herzl's successor," he was told.

Then Dr. Weizmann traveled throughout the United States, sometimes making two or three speeches a day. Wherever he went, he was given an enthusiastic welcome. He asked for funds to build up Palestine, and the Americans contributed generously.

"A country is acquired in the pain of struggle against all obstacles," Dr. Weizmann told his American audiences. "In Palestine, we know the pain of drying up the swamps, laying the roads, putting up tents, and fighting the natural elements. And that is what is meant by the homeland of a people."

While in America, Dr. Weizmann heard that Haj Amin was back in Jerusalem. He had been pardoned and had been reappointed mufti of Jerusalem by the British high commissioner.

"This is not good news for either the Jews or the Arabs," Dr. Weizmann commented.

From America, the Weizmanns traveled to Italy, to France, and to Germany, trying to gain wide support and additional funds for the Jewish national home. Dr. Weizmann had no time for chemistry now.

In Germany, Professor Albert Einstein backed the Zionist project, but most German Jews refused to believe Dr. Weizmann when he told them, "You need Palestine as much as anyone else."

They scoffed, "We are Germans, and we are safe here. We don't need any other country." Their attitude was exactly as he remembered it during his student years in Pfungstadt.

Dr. Weizmann traveled on to South Africa, and then once more to Palestine. There he heard that the mufti was using his religious office for political propaganda and terrorism.

"Twenty million Jews are pouring into the country to uproot you," Haj Amin told the Arab press.

Palestine was attracting more and more Arabs from other areas, for the swamps that Jewish pioneers had bought and drained were now productive farmlands. Palestine, the wasteland, was becoming a desirable area, and the property cultivated by Jews seemed most desirable of all.

Haj Amin kept saying the Jews were taking the best land. He neglected to add that the land was not the best until the Jews made it so.

When an anti-Zionist British general in command of Jaffa stated, "Should there be a slaughter, I'll stand at my window and watch," Haj Amin gleefully proclaimed, "The government is with us."

Shortly afterward, mobs of Arabs attacked Jews in Jaffa, and ninety-five were killed. Palestinian Jews realized that they had to rely on themselves for self-defense just as the Russian Jews had. They organized a home guard called the *Haganah*.

The Haganah became a secret army that drilled by night, and by day wielded the hammers, picks, and shovels used in building a nation. Its officers and troops were men who once fought alongside the British at Gallipoli and Jerusalem.

When the Jews let it be known that they would defend themselves, a period of peace followed, bringing order and growth. Arabs from neighboring Syria and

Lebanon, attracted by improved living conditions, came freely across the border into Palestine.

Meanwhile, the Zionists were purchasing all the land they could afford for their settlements. They bought swamps, deserted lands, and stony hills for their *kibbutzim*, communes in which the Jews shared the farm work and the profits equally, and for their *moshavs*, cooperative farms whose members joined together to buy supplies and sell crops. Dr. Weizmann believed that the land must be bought legally and at a fair price, and the Zionists followed this practice.

However, every improvement the Jews made raised the price of nearby land; the Arab landowners lost no time in taking advantage of the rising demand. Dr. Weizmann had hoped that in accordance with the mandate, the British government would give the Zionists stretches of land that were government property. But he was disappointed in this hope.

"I was wrong," Dr. Weizmann admitted. "We shall have to buy every bit of land needed for our colonization on the open market."

Dr. Weizmann divided his time between England and Palestine. He was in London when the Parliament held debates on Palestine. A great volume of criticism was directed against the mandate, with some members of Parliament even moving for the repeal of the Balfour Declaration. The government outlined its current policies in a White Paper, which was published in June

1922. It was called the Churchill White Paper after Winston Churchill, who was secretary of state for war and Near Eastern affairs.

Although the Churchill White Paper affirmed the Balfour Declaration, it also limited the area in which the Balfour Declaration would apply. The part of Palestine that lay east of the Jordan River was removed

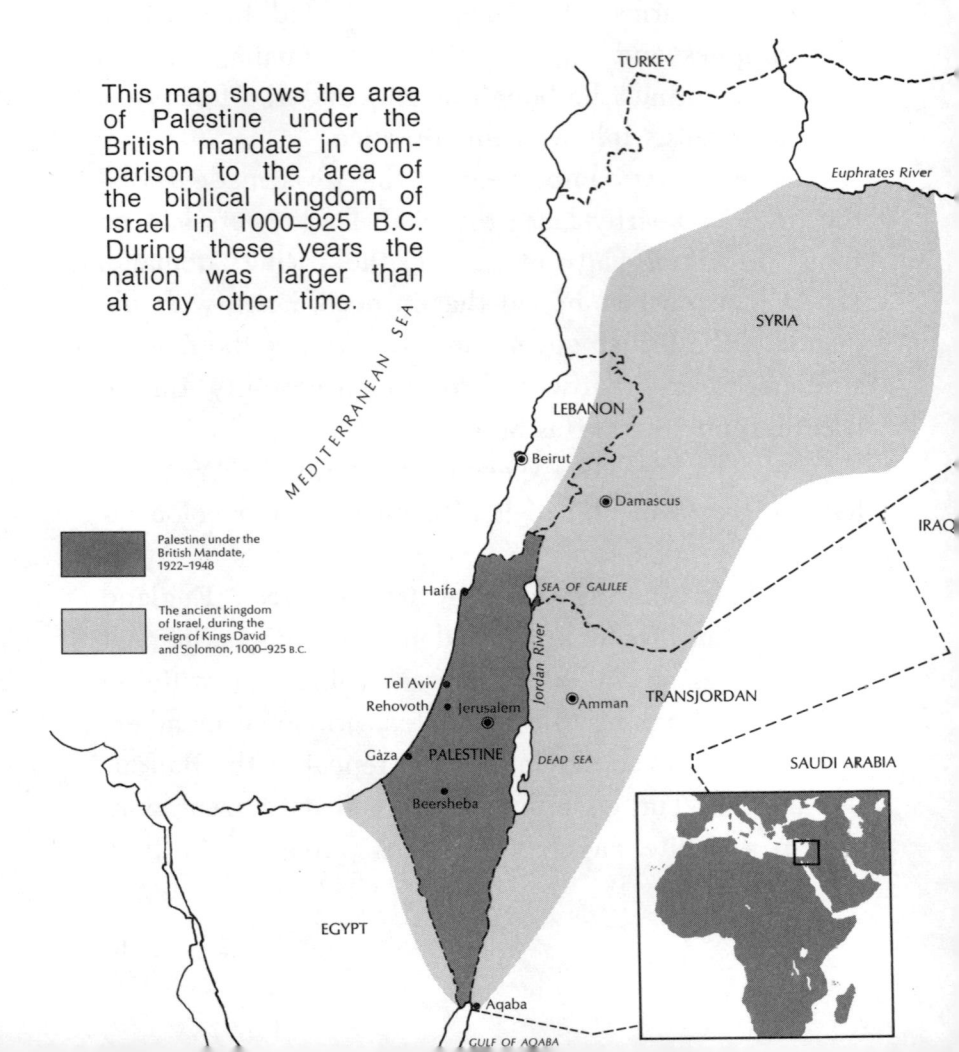

This map shows the area of Palestine under the British mandate in comparison to the area of the biblical kingdom of Israel in 1000–925 B.C. During these years the nation was larger than at any other time.

from the mandate and became the kingdom of Transjordan. Feisal's brother was installed as its ruler. Feisal himself became the new king of Iraq.

Palestine was now one-fifth of the size that was shown on maps prior to World War I. Only in this fraction of the original territory could a Jewish national home be established.

"We have no choice; we must accept this," Dr. Weizmann told his Zionist colleagues, "though I must admit having some qualms."

Dr. Weizmann was in Jerusalem on April 1, 1925, for the "opening ceremonies" of the Hebrew University. Both Vera and Benjy were with him.

Dr. Weizmann decided to inspect the site of the ceremonies the day before the opening. Driving from Jerusalem to Mount Scopus, Dr. Weizmann noted the narrow road. "It's so narrow, nobody will be able to turn around," he commented.

"Don't worry, chief," said a member of the committee which had made the arrangements. "It will work out. Everyone will be going in the same direction; they won't have to turn around."

When they arrived on Mount Scopus, Dr. Weizmann took one look at the speakers' platform. "It's only a little wooden bridge!" he exclaimed. "My blood runs cold with fear; what if something gives way?"

"This platform can hold 250 people safely," the committee man said.

117

"They could all fall down that rocky gorge," Dr. Weizmann worried.

"We can prove how strong this platform is," the committee man replied.

The 200 young pioneers who had built the platform climbed on top of it and energetically danced the *hora*, a Jewish circle dance. Dr. Weizmann expected the platform to give way any moment and to see the young people hurtling into the chasm. To his relief, however, the platform held.

"I have to admit that it seems like a solid platform," Dr. Weizmann said when the dance was done. "But what if someone sabotages it during the night? You know these ceremonies have been advertised."

"We will guard it," the pioneers promised. So the night before the opening ceremonies, the builders stayed on Mount Scopus and guarded their platform.

When Dr. Weizmann returned to Jerusalem, he met the train that brought Lord Balfour, now seventy-seven years old. The elderly statesman stepped slowly off the train. Dr. Weizmann took him by the hand, and bade him, "Welcome, in the name of the Jewish nation, to the Jewish National Home."

Lord Balfour clasped Dr. Weizmann's hand. "We are here together for this great occasion."

"This is the first time in two thousand years," Dr. Weizmann said, "that the Jewish people have been able to be hosts to such an honored guest."

The ceremony was scheduled for the afternoon. Among the 12,000 guests were the British military in their dress uniforms, Arab sheiks in their most beautiful robes, and the pioneer Jewish youth in simple clothing of blue and white, the colors of the Jewish flag.

When Lord Balfour, attired as chancellor of Edinburgh University, arrived, he was greeted by a ringing ovation.

Dr. Weizmann sat at the center of the platform, surrounded by Lord Balfour, the chief rabbis of Jerusalem, England, and France, distinguished scholars and writers, and British generals. As Dr. Weizmann moved forward to speak, the crimson gown of the Doctorate of Science hung upon him like a prophet's mantle. He glanced momentarily around him. Behind him dropped an abyss, a ten-mile plunge of white rock and gray sand to the Jordan River. Thirty miles away, across the chasm, the cliffs of Moab burned purple and bronze in the sunlight.

Dr. Weizmann declared:

> What we are inaugurating here today is a Hebrew University. The university, while maintaining the highest scientific level, must be rendered accessible to all classes of people. The workman and farm laborer must be able to find here a possibility of continuing and completing their education in their free hours. The doors of our li-

A dream comes true—the dedication of the Hebrew University in 1925. Dr. Weizmann (left) watches as Lord Balfour speaks at the colorful ceremony on Mount Scopus.

braries, lecture rooms, and laboratories must be opened widely to them all. Thus the university will exercise its beneficial influence on the nation as a whole...

Dr. Weizmann paused for a moment, then said, "A university is nothing if it is not universal. Within the precincts of this school, all creeds and races will, I hope, be united in the great task of searching for truth, in restoring to Palestine the thriving civilization which it once enjoyed."

After the crowds had dispersed, Dr. Weizmann showed Lord Balfour and a reporter around the university. Dr. Weizmann pointed to the Microbiological Institute, which was in a handsome building. He showed them the library—stacked in a temporary shelter—a few classrooms, and a powerhouse.

"This is all we have now," Dr. Weizmann said. "Later there will be a college of arts and letters here." He pointed to this area. "There will be the college of science," he said as he indicated another area. Dr. Weizmann also told Lord Balfour that the Hebrew language, dead for centuries, had been revived so that Jews from various nations could communicate with one another.

"This is the beginning," Dr. Weizmann said, "and this is the high point of my life."

13. Danger Looms

Even as Dr. Weizmann took pleasure in seeing the new university take shape, trouble was brewing. In trying to establish a Jewish national home in Palestine, the Jews had become a pawn in Great Britain's struggle to maintain world power.

New British leaders were more interested in securing the friendship of Arabs in surrounding countries than in upholding commitments to the Jews in Palestine. The British needed oil from Arab lands; they needed bases on Arab soil; and the British Empire was dependent on the trade which flowed through the Suez Canal.

It was felt by many British leaders that they could make their position in the Arab world more secure by giving in to the demands of the Arabs in Palestine. This feeling was often reflected in the attitudes of British officials in Palestine toward Jewish settlers.

Nevertheless, Dr. Weizmann and other Zionist leaders continued with the day-to-day work of building the national home.

In the summer of 1929, a meeting of the Jewish Agency, the body officially representing Jews engaged in this work under the British mandate, was held in Zurich, Switzerland. It was attended by such great men as Professor Albert Einstein, Leon Blum, who was to become premier of France, and Felix Warburg of the American banking family. Under Dr. Weizmann's leadership, Jews of varying political beliefs had joined to support the Jewish national home.

The publicity about this meeting aroused Haj Amin once more. From his Jerusalem office, he again spread word in the Palestine mosques that "world Jewish conspirators" had decided to destroy the Moslems' holy Mosque of Omar.

Two days after the Zurich meeting ended, Dr. Weizmann received a telegram from England which began: "The Under Secretary of State regrets to announce that 150 Jews were killed." Stirred to a holy war, the Arabs had fallen upon Jews in the old religious quarters of Jerusalem, Safed, and Hebron. The new settlements, where the Haganah men stood guard, were not attacked.

Back in England, Dr. Weizmann was invited to Saint James' Palace to address the staffs of both the Colonial and Foreign Offices.

Dr. Weizmann said, "I think His Majesty's government must be well aware that there is only one quarter from which disaffection, disorder, and violence, and massacre have originated. We Jews do not massacre; we were the victims of murderous onslaught. Not one Arab leader has raised his voice against the inhuman treatment meted out to the unfortunate victims."

After the session, a prominent member of the British government remarked, "What we have just heard concerns England as much as it concerns the Jews."

Nevertheless, in the fall of 1930 the British government issued the Passfield White Paper which declared publicly its intention to suspend immigration, introduce restrictive land legislation, and limit the authority of the Jewish Agency.

Dr. Weizmann, in his official capacity as president of the World Zionist Organization, called on its author, Lord Passfield, colonial secretary in the Labor government, and protested. "This White Paper," he said, "is a direct violation of the Mandate given by the League of Nations to Britain." He reminded Passfield of the Balfour Declaration and Britain's past promises. But Lord Passfield only tried to make a joke of the situation.

"I regret to see that you deal with promises frivolously," Dr. Weizmann said. "I can't see how you, as a British patriot, don't realize the moral implications of promises given by your government."

Lord Passfield still would not repudiate the White Paper. Dr. Weizmann stalked out of his office angrily.

Now Dr. Weizmann drove himself harder than ever. When Ramsay MacDonald was elected prime minister, Dr. Weizmann persuaded him to stand behind the Balfour Declaration.

Ramsay MacDonald wrote a letter to the House of Commons, agreeing to carry out the promises of the Balfour Declaration. The limitations set upon immigration in the Passfield White Paper were lifted.

Dr. Weizmann was satisfied with the letter, but many of his fellow Zionists were not. They said, "A letter isn't really official."

"When the prime minister writes a letter to the House of Commons, it is official," Dr. Weizmann replied.

Other Zionists, however, kept urging Dr. Weizmann to get another White Paper issued. Dr. Weizmann refused, for he knew that by writing the letter, the British leaders were saving face. Britain would look indecisive in the eyes of the world if one White Paper contradicted another.

At the Zionist Congress held in Basel in 1931, the delegates debated the pros and cons of the MacDonald letter.

"We must continue to rely on the British," Dr. Weizmann stated firmly.

Ben Gurion, now a leader of the Zionist labor party in Palestine, had lost patience with the British. He accused Dr. Weizmann of putting British politics above Jewish needs.

"Let us put it to a vote," Dr. Weizmann suggested.

When the roll was taken, the Zionist Congress had voted no confidence in Dr. Weizmann's leadership.

"Since that is the sentiment of the majority, I hereby

tender my resignation as president of the World Zionist Organization," Dr. Weizmann said with dignity.

Still, he was unhappy. He had worked ceaselessly for the Jewish national home, and now his fellow Zionists voted no confidence in him.

"Chaimchik," Vera said, "this is your great opportunity to take a long vacation. Let's go on a holiday."

They decided to revisit Switzerland, which they had loved as students. They had just reached Geneva, however, when a telegram arrived. The English Zionists wanted him to represent them at a high-level meeting of the British government.

"This is your vacation, Chaim," Vera said. "Let them get someone else."

"But, Vera, I cannot give up now. If they need me, I must go." Dr. Weizmann cut short his vacation and returned to England where he was invited to serve as president of the English Zionists. He accepted happily because the job was not as demanding as the presidency of the world organization.

With more leisure time, Dr. Weizmann decided to return to his beloved chemistry. Although he had not even been inside a laboratory for thirteen years, he stayed up late night after night reading reports and chemistry journals in an attempt to catch up with the latest developments in the sciences. He worked for a time with a noted German scientist who was visiting London. Even Michael, who was majoring in physics at Cambridge, tried to help by discussing his work with his father.

When he felt ready, Dr. Weizmann established a laboratory of his own in London. His days fell into an orderly pattern.

He could not ignore, however, the bad news from Germany. A few years earlier an obscure politician named Adolf Hitler had written a book called *Mein Kampf*, an outline of his political beliefs. Hitler believed that the Germans were a master race and preached hatred against the Jews. His followers, the members of the National Socialist party, or Nazis, had beaten German Jews, robbed them, and smashed their stores. The Nazis had grown stronger as the years went by. The German government tried to stop them, but their numbers increased until the Nazi party had become the largest party in the Reichstag, the German parliament. In 1933, Adolf Hitler became chancellor of Germany.

German Jews, who a few years ago had felt safe in their German citizenship, were frightened. The Jewish Agency responded to the critical situation by setting up the Central Bureau for the Settlement of the German Jews to help them leave Germany.

Dr. Weizmann was named chairman of this bureau. He had no particular qualifications for this work, but the need was urgent. The human suffering was so great and the men and women so pathetic in their misfortunes that Dr. Weizmann felt he must do the best he could.

"Hitler means every word he wrote in *Mein Kampf*," he told the German Jews. "Get out of Germany immediately."

Some heeded his warning, but there were many more who remained. "Our contributions to the fatherland are outstanding," many professors, scientists, and doctors said. "Surely the Nazis will not bother us."

"This is the saddest time of my life," Dr. Weizmann told Vera. "I tell the German Jews to run for their lives, and so many of them will not listen. How can I save them if they are not willing to be saved?"

In 1935, Dr. Weizmann was once again elected president of the World Zionist Organization at its biannual meeting. That year 62,000 Jews, mostly from Germany, left Europe to settle in Palestine.

Two years later, Chaim and Vera Weizmann built a home on land purchased from the Aaron Eisenberg family in Palestine. They planned to live there most of the time, but they kept their London home as Dr. Weizmann was frequently called to England.

Vera chose the site. "I am buying the view," she said, pointing toward Jerusalem and the Judean hills. She liked the site too, for it was close to Chaim's laboratory in the new scientific institute which had been established there. When he was in Palestine, Dr. Weizmann went to his laboratory everyday.

Vera worked with the architect in planning the house. When it was finished, Dr. Weizmann was especially pleased with the library with its open fireplace. Here he could keep all his books and read in quiet.

Dr. Weizmann, however, found few opportunities for quiet study, for Palestine was a land of turmoil. He received all the reports on Arab terrorism waged against the Jews, the British government, and also against a large number of Arabs. When the local Arabs refused to join him, Haj Amin brought in a gang of killers from Syria. Most of the Palestinian Arabs preferred to live in peace with their Jewish neighbors, but if they did not shelter the mufti's hired gunmen, they themselves would be killed. Haj Amin also took

As many as 22 people were killed and 130 injured in this anti-Jewish riot in Jaffa in the 1930s.

advantage of the unstable political situation to settle accounts with his Arab political opponents. Haj Amin's mercenaries slaughtered 136 prominent Palestinian Arabs who opposed him.

In warring against the Jews, Haj Amin's men cut down trees planted by the colonists, destroyed their homes and wells, as well as oil pipelines. Because of the Haganah's alertness, the loss of Jewish life was kept down.

Dr. Weizmann was pleased that the Haganah followed the Zionist policy of fighting only in self-defense. One group of Haganah men, however, was not satisfied with this strategy. They had lost brothers and fathers in the Arab attacks. Now they formed a new force called the *Irgun Zvai Leumi;* they sought out Arabs in their hideouts and struck against them there. Dr. Weizmann urged all Palestinian Jews to use self-restraint and to work through the Haganah, but the Irgun refused.

In July 1937, Dr. Weizmann was in London when the Peel Report was issued. The year before, the British government had sent a commission under Lord Peel to Palestine to make a thorough study of conditions there and to recommend ways of pacifying the peoples. The Peel Report acknowledged the high quality of work done by the Jews, but it declared the mandate unworkable, and proposed the partition of Palestine into three sections: an Arab state, a Jewish state, and a British-administered area.

For Dr. Weizmann, this report was both heartbreaking and hopeful. It was the first time a British government agency had recommended a Jewish state. But at the same time, only a tiny area was being offered to the Jews. Dr. Weizmann laughed ironically when he saw a cartoon in a London newspaper; it showed a Jewish pioneer standing on a tiny platform, with a hammer and a scythe in his hands. The tag line read, "Standing room only."

Dr. Weizmann took the Peel Report to the twentieth Zionist Congress, which met in Basel in August. This partition proposal divided the Zionist delegates and reminded Dr. Weizmann of the Uganda schism of more than thirty years before. He had to convince his fellow Zionists to work together now that Arab terrorists were plaguing Palestine, and the Nazis were unleashing other terrors.

When Dr. Weizmann rose to make his report, the huge hall, packed with delegates and visitors, was tense with expectation. He described the Jewish problem as part of the world problem; he told of the complicated economic and political forces entangling the world's statesmen and the helplessness of far more powerful peoples. Against this background he drew the picture of the Jews who were trapped and desperate in Nazi Germany. A Jewish state, however small, could control its own immigration and thus provide refuge for these Jews.

When he finished speaking, someone asked, "How many Jews have to be transferred from Europe and settled in Palestine in order to meet the situation created by the Nazis?"

Dr. Weizmann answered, "A minimum of two million of our younger generation."

"What about the older generation?" someone asked.

"They will be ground into economic dust," Dr. Weizmann replied.

The poignancy of those words deeply stirred his listeners; a murmur ran through the crowded hall. Dr. Weizmann had brought home to the Zionists the perilous situation of the Jews.

When the time came to vote on the Peel Report, the Zionist Congress empowered "the Executive to enter into negotiations with a view to ascertaining the precise terms of His Majesty's Government for the proposed establishment of a Jewish State."

Back in London, Dr. Weizmann told British officials that the Peel proposal might offer a "possibility of coming to terms with the Arabs."

When Haj Amin heard of the Peel Report, he immediately opposed it. He refused to negotiate at all; he wanted the entire country, even the Jewish sections, to be under Arab control.

In the meantime, Haj Amin sent a representative to confer with Germany. In exchange for "ideological and material support," Haj Amin proposed helping Germany by creating a sympathetic atmosphere for Germany that would be useful in case of war—by boycotting Jewish merchandise, by battling the formation of a Jewish state in Palestine, and by organizing terrorist actions in all territories and colonies inhabited by Arabs or other Moslems.

About the same time, Haj Amin began broadcasting anti-British propaganda in Arabic throughout the Mideast.

At long last, what had been clear to Dr. Weizmann for some time now also became clear to the British government. Then a British official in Palestine was murdered by the mufti's men. That was the last straw. The British decided to arrest the mufti. Many of the mufti's cohorts were caught, but the mufti himself, dressed as a woman, escaped from the British mandated territory into Syria. There he continued to work with the Nazis.

While still in London, Dr. Weizmann attended the wedding of his son Benjy, a businessman, to Maidie Pomerantz, a medical student. Dr. Weizmann and Vera escorted their son to the wedding canopy and watched Maidie, dressed in traditional white, walk up the aisle to the accompaniment of violins playing old melodies.

"It doesn't seem so long ago that we were the newlyweds," Vera said, and wiped away a happy tear.

Chaim Weizmann squeezed his wife's hand in silent agreement.

14. Chemist in World War II

Back in Palestine, Dr. Weizmann listened to the news on the radio and grew more despondent. The Nazis were ransacking Jewish homes; they arrested Jews suddenly, simply because they were Jews, and carted them off to concentration camps, where they suffered torture and death.

Then in March 1938, Nazi forces occupied Austria and annexed the country. Dr. Weizmann was appalled that Neville Chamberlain, the new British prime minister, had participated in the Munich Pact, which gave Germany a large part of Czechoslovakia.

The international situation had changed radically, and Dr. Weizmann knew that for the Jews, for millions of them, it would be terrible.

Now when thousands of Jewish men, women, and children were desperately trying to escape the Nazis, Chamberlain's government proposed a new White Paper, which would limit Jewish immigration into Palestine to 75,000 during the next five years and stop the sale of land to Jews. It also promised Palestine independence in ten years with a permanently frozen population in the proportion of two Arabs to every Jew. This proposal canceled the Balfour Declaration and, in effect, the recommendation of the Peel Commission for the partition of Palestine.

"I can scarcely believe this," Dr. Weizmann cried upon hearing about it. "Though after seeing what happened to poor Czechoslovakia, nothing should surprise me."

Dr. Weizmann felt compelled to speak up. He traveled to London, made an appointment with the prime minister, and went to 10 Downing Street.

"There are 400,000 Jews in Palestine now," Dr. Weizmann stated. "The British promised them a national home, and they are developing that home with the sweat of their brows. There is plenty of room for the Arabs and Jews to live side by side, even if many more Jewish settlers arrive. If your government keeps its word and handles both sides fairly, good relations between Jews and Arabs can be established."

The prime minister sat like a marble statue and said not one word. To Dr. Weizmann it seemed obvious that Chamberlain was bent on appeasing the Arabs just as he had appeased Hitler.

Dr. Weizmann left the prime minister, still sitting silently. At a crucial period in history, Britain was led by a man who saw nothing.

Several days later the White Paper of 1939, which had been proposed, was indeed issued.

When Dr. Weizmann attended the twenty-first Zionist Congress in Geneva in August 1939, he found a cloud of fear hanging over the delegates. Little business was conducted. The only important vote taken was the condemnation of the British White Paper.

During the Congress, a telegram arrived for Dr. Weizmann. Germany and Russia had signed a treaty of mutual assistance. "The Jewish calamity has merged with the world calamity," Dr. Weizmann said, after reading the telegram aloud.

When he rose to bid good-bye to the delegates, Dr. Weizmann quoted from an ancient Jewish prayer: "Who shall live and who shall die, who in time and who before his time, who shall die by the sword and who shall die by hunger, we do not know, but we part hoping that we shall meet again. Whether we shall, that is no longer in our hands."

When Dr. Weizmann stepped down from the rostrum, he shook the hand of each delegate who planned to return to family and home in eastern Europe. He said, "May God be with you."

A few days later, on September 1, Hitler's armies overran Poland. A cold chill ran down Dr. Weizmann's spine for he realized what Nazi occupation meant to Polish Jews.

"At last!" Dr. Weizmann murmured when he heard the prime minister warn Hitler to withdraw from Poland. "Chamberlain realizes Britain may be next."

Hitler paid no attention to the British warning. His armies penetrated farther into Poland, and his Luftwaffe, the German air force, bombed the cities.

Great Britain and France declared war against Germany.

At the outbreak of war, Palestine's Arab leaders openly backed Hitler. Fighting for its life, Britain rushed troops to the Middle East to crack down on Arab activities against the Allies. The mufti fled to Germany; there he became a Nazi propagandist and advocated mass extermination of the Jews.

Now Dr. Weizmann was torn between loyalty to England, his home for 35 years, and bitterness at Chamberlain's betrayal of Jewish hopes for a national home. There was little choice for Dr. Weizmann since Hitler's announced policy was the extermination of the Jews. The important thing now was to defeat Hitler, so Dr. Weizmann tried to forget the White Paper and work for the British.

"I like what Ben Gurion said," Dr. Weizmann told Vera. "We will fight the war as if there were no White Paper, and we will fight the White Paper as if there were no war."

Dr. Weizmann's sons agreed with him. When the White Paper of 1939 was first issued, Benjy and Michael passionately declared they would never defend Great Britain, but now the two joined the British armed forces. Benjy served with an antiartillery unit guarding Kent.

Benjamin Weizmann (left) and Michael Weizmann (right) in their wartime uniforms.

Sometimes his battalion was under fire for days at a stretch as the Luftwaffe flew over. During such periods, the men went without sleep, food, or drink. The bombardment was nerve shattering. After a half year of service, Benjy was sent to the hospital suffering from shock.

Michael, newly graduated from Cambridge and a brilliant young physicist at the age of twenty-two, joined the Royal Air Force. He flew on patrol duty above the tossing seas, sometimes south to Gibralter, sometimes west toward Iceland, and usually at night.

Michael visited his parents in London whenever he got a leave. Sometimes it was only for a couple of hours.

These visits were a source of joy and sadness for them, for he no sooner arrived than it was time to leave. Often Dr. Weizmann walked with Michael into the blacked-out streets until Michael said good-bye and disappeared into the dark.

Dr. Weizmann was fighting in his own way for Great Britain. Winston Churchill, who had succeeded Neville Chamberlain as prime minister, appointed Dr. Weizmann as honorary chemical adviser to the Ministry of Supply. Dr. Weizmann was given a laboratory, a staff of scientists, and laboratory workers.

Dr. Weizmann tried to forget his disappointment over broken British promises as he worked to create chemical substitutes for necessary supplies cut off by the Nazis. Heads of British wartime offices came to him with their problems. One rather jolly caller was the one-time trade-union leader, Ernest Bevin, who as minister of labor sought help in obtaining fuel for factories.

Vera Weizmann also helped by serving as a physician in a bomb shelter. Every night she went to a cellar in the London slums where 2,000 people sought safety from the Nazi blitz. Besides treating those who had been wounded by broken glass or who were in a state of shock, Vera tried to cheer up the people in the dismal, crowded cellar. She often wound up a phonograph and played records to drown out the sound of falling bombs.

Chaim Weizmann worked day and night. He stayed in his laboratory working when he was supposed to be taking shelter. This saved his life, for one night the shelter to which he was assigned suffered a direct hit; fifteen people were killed.

Soon one task crowded out all others. It became vital to develop a synthetic rubber to substitute for natural rubber, as the Nazis had cut off Britain's Malay supply.

Dr. Weizmann took time off from his experiments, however, to plead with British leaders, "Let more Jews into Palestine; save their lives."

The British were following the White Paper to the letter and allowed only 1,500 refugees into Palestine each month. All others were turned away even though it meant that they had no place to go. "A law is a law," the British said.

"Not when it is immoral," Dr. Weizmann retorted.

Dr. Weizmann knew that a network of Jewish agents was working in every port of the Western world; these agents raised funds, bought and chartered ships, and gathered together Jews to make the technically illegal entry into Palestine. By the thousands these agents smuggled the desperate Jews out of Nazi territories and transported them across international boundaries to ports where they could embark for Palestine.

Many were captured by the British as their overcrowded ships, often leftover hulks waiting for the ship-breaker, approached the Palestine coast. These refugees were sent to British detention centers. Those who were able to evade the British blockade were unloaded into tiny fishing vessels under the command of the Haganah and taken to shore. Once on land, the refugees were dispersed among the Jewish settlements so they could not be traced by the British.

The refugee ships kept sailing, although some were little better than leaky tubs. One such ship, the *Salvador*, sank with 300 aboard before it reached Palestine. Another ship, the *Struma*, with 769 passengers aboard, was held in the Turkish port of Istanbul while attempts were made to obtain entrance permits to Palestine for its passengers. When the British refused, Turkish authorities forced the ship back to sea. It soon sank, probably torpedoed by a Nazi submarine.

World opinion was shocked, but the British held fast to the immigration quotas set by the White Paper of 1939. Despite their anger, however, Jews of the free world continued to fight fiercely for the Allied cause.

Early in 1942, Dr. Weizmann was asked to go to the United States, an ally in the war, and work there on the problem of producing synthetic rubber.

Dr. Weizmann dropped in at 10 Downing Street to bid Churchill good-bye. As Churchill chewed his cigar, he said, "I have a plan. After the war, Britain and America will recognize Jewish claims in Palestine."

Dr. Weizmann sighed. He had heard so many British promises in the past. He hoped that the British would keep this one.

Dr. and Mrs. Weizmann went to the airport in Bristol, England, to board their plane for America. As they waited, Dr. Weizmann was summoned to the telephone. He returned to Vera looking crumpled and old.

Vera knew there had been bad news. She asked, "Is he dead or missing?"

"Michael is missing," he answered.

The Weizmanns canceled their flight and took the first train back to London where Benjy and Maidie met them. They drove silently to the hotel. Friends dropped in to shake their hands in mute sympathy.

Before long, the Weizmanns learned about Michael's last flight. Michael had engaged two Nazi gunboats over the English Channel and was shot down. He radioed for help from his stricken aircraft, but no other plane could be spared for his rescue in the rage of battle. By the time the attack was over, Michael's signals had stopped.

The Weizmanns prayed that their son was alive. "Perhaps he was taken prisoner of war," they consoled each other as they waited for further word. That word never came.

This personal loss wore Dr. Weizmann down. He, who usually stood tall and straight, now stooped.

The Weizmanns lingered in London, vainly hoping for news of Michael. Then with aching hearts they left for America.

There Dr. Weizmann hoped to plunge immediately into the production of synthetic rubber from butyl alcohol, a substance which could be derived from fermented grain. The United States government had already engaged oil companies to produce synthetic rubber from oil, however, so Dr. Weizmann met delays and opposition.

Dr. Weizmann struggled for some months to achieve recognition, but finally he became discouraged. He turned his process over to a Philadelphia firm, which later successfully produced synthetic rubber according to his formula. Dr. and Mrs. Weizmann then decided to return to England. They had been in the United States for a year and a half.

In London, Dr. Weizmann called on Churchill and again asked for a retraction of the White Paper.

Churchill was still seeking Arab friendship, however, and insisted that any change would have to come after the war.

Dr. Weizmann now began to long for his home in Rehovoth. He had not been in Palestine since those hectic days before the White Paper of 1939 was issued. He wanted to be in his home for his seventieth birthday. Although the war made traveling dangerous, he and Vera managed to return safely to Rehovoth.

143

Palestinian friends staged a week of festivities in honor of Dr. Weizmann's birthday. The Jewish Brigade, volunteers who had served in the British forces, paraded before him, and a reception of 600 people was held in Jerusalem.

For some time Dr. Weizmann's eyesight had been deteriorating. In the spring of 1945, the Weizmanns returned to England, where he underwent several painful operations on his eyes.

As Dr. Weizmann recuperated, he rejoiced to hear of the American and British armies sweeping into Germany. Before summer, the Nazi armies collapsed.

Now the full horror of the Nazi reign was revealed, as Allied soldiers and journalists saw the Nazi concentration camps for the first time. They saw the cattle cars in which Jews had been transported to the camps, the gas chambers in which so many of them had perished, and the piles of bodies still waiting to be cremated.

The war was over, but the Jewish population of Europe had been reduced by six million. It had been worse than Dr. Weizmann or anyone had foreseen.

15. Let the Gates Open

When the Japanese surrendered in August 1945, World War II was over, but the human suffering was not. There were 30,000 emaciated Jews in concentration camps with no place to go. Chaim Weizmann sought help for these tragic remnants of European Jewry who had no desire to return to the lands that had abused them. Military authorities set up Displaced Persons' Camps for them until permanent homes could be found. The camps' population increased as thousands of Polish Jews fled from new attacks by the Polish people.

Once more Dr. Weizmann called British attention to Palestine as a haven and was once more told that the White Paper was still in effect.

Then Churchill, who had led his nation through its darkest hour, was voted out of office, and the Labor party was voted in. Dr. Weizmann remembered how, before elections, the Labor party had attacked the White Paper as an evil document and declared itself in favor of opening Palestine to every Jew who sought entry.

So Dr. Weizmann called on Ernest Bevin, the affable man who had sought his help during the war. Bevin, now Britain's foreign minister, regulated immigration into Palestine.

No longer bothering to be jolly, Bevin flatly refused to honor campaign promises. "The Jews," he told Dr. Weizmann, "should stay in Germany and the countries of their birth and help rebuild them."

"Do you really believe that?" Dr. Weizmann asked incredulously. "Knowing as you do that six million of them were slaughtered, and that the minds of the Germans and others are poisoned with hatred, do you believe that?"

Bevin shrugged. "The British government," he said in a tone of finality, "will follow the provisions set forth in the White Paper; that allows 1,500 Jews to enter Palestine each month, you know."

"Mr. Bevin, when you needed my help to supply fuel for the factories, you did not set any quotas. Why would you now set a quota on rescuing my people?" Dr. Weizmann said, but Bevin remained unmoved.

Dr. Weizmann reported this conversation to David Ben Gurion, who had grown from pioneer to labor leader to chairman of the Jewish Agency. In Palestine, the Jews immediately staged a protest strike. Everyone stopped work, and peaceful meetings were held in cities. Although Dr. Weizmann and other Jewish leaders were opposed to violence, certain Jews, angry with Britain's many broken treaties, broke into the British government offices in Tel Aviv, set fires, smashed windows, and destroyed important papers.

The British were not moved. They continued their policy of turning away from Palestine shiploads of dazed survivors from Dachau and other concentration camps. The British held thousands of Jewish refugees behind barbed wire in a detention center on Cyprus.

Daily the relationship between the British and Palestinian Jews worsened. The Haganah continued helping the sad survivors in spite of British rules. Out of a population of 700,000 Jews in Palestine, 10 percent were now in the Haganah, an army without uniform or insignia.

These survivors of the Nazi death camps appeal to British soldiers to permit them to enter Palestine.

When the Haganah managed to bring in a ship secretly, Palestinian Jews mingled with the refugees so that British immigration officers could not tell who belonged in Palestine and who did not.

The Haganah stepped up its purchase of old freighters and other decrepit ships, recruited sailors, and transported refugees waiting in Mediterranean seaports to Palestine.

British warships intercepted many of the converted ships and took the refugees back to Displaced Persons' Camps in Europe or to the British detention center on Cyprus. One ship, the *Exodus*, was boarded by the British while it was still at sea and taken to Haifa. When the refugees refused to move onto British ships, British sailors attacked them with tear gas and beat them into unconsciousness. Once aboard the British prison ships, they were returned to Germany.

Frustrated by the British, the Irgun and the Stern Gang, extremist groups that advocated violence, attacked the British. They blew up the King David Hotel, British headquarters in Jerusalem, and most of the ninety-one persons killed were British.

Dr. Weizmann and other Jewish leaders pleaded for patience, but the Stern Gang felt that patience had gotten few refugees into Palestine.

Americans who had helped defeat the Nazis and had seen the German death camps were intensely interested in the fate of the survivors. At this time President

Harry S. Truman cabled the British, requesting them to allow 100,000 Jews into Palestine immediately.

Still the British hesitated, so President Truman suggested the formation of an Anglo-American commission. This commission took a poll of Jews in the Displaced Persons' Camps and found that the vast majority wanted to go to one place—Palestine.

The commission then visited Palestine to see whether the small country could absorb so many Jews. Dr. Weizmann met the commission on its arrival. He escorted the members to areas that the Jewish pioneers had watered and planted, making the desert bloom.

When the Anglo-American Commission saw how much of the country was still uninhabited, they realized there was plenty of room for more Jews in Palestine. The commission urged the British government to admit 100,000 Jews immediately.

The British government, however, refused to follow the recommendation. It clung stubbornly to the White Paper. The Arabs still did not want the Jewish population to grow, and the British did not want to lose their power in the area by antagonizing the Arabs.

In Egypt, the mufti who had worked hand in hand with Hitler, was now organizing attacks against the Palestinian Jews. Dr. Weizmann heard rumors that the British were helping the mufti!

Dr. Weizmann felt bitter, but he would not give up now. In June of 1946 the cornerstone of the Weizmann

Institute of Science was laid near his home in Rehovoth. The new institute, named in honor of Dr. Weizmann, included the scientific institute at Rehovoth, which he had established so many years before. Soon afterward he went to Geneva for the twenty-second Zionist Congress. It was the Zionists' first important meeting since the war. When Dr. Weizmann stood up to conduct the meeting, he saw the empty seats where the Polish Jews once sat; he saw the empty section where the German and French Jews usually sat. More than a third of the world's Jewish population had been killed by the Nazis.

Dr. Weizmann faced his people and asked the Congress to send representatives to a forthcoming conference in London, called by the British government. There the fate of Palestine would be discussed once more.

"How can we trust the British?" the delegates shouted. "They make promises to us out of one side of their mouth, and make promises to the Arabs out of the other side."

Dr. Weizmann pleaded with the delegates, "However frustrating, we must not break off negotiations with the British."

This Congress, though, consisted of younger men new to Zionism. They had no tradition of trusting the British as Dr. Weizmann had done through the years.

Moreover, Ben Gurion, the spokesman for the

Palestinian Jews, was calling for forceful, militant action.

Chaim Weizmann believed that a vote against representation at the London Conference implied lack of confidence in his leadership. He called for a vote. The World Zionist Organization voted against him. Dr. Weizmann stepped down from the podium and took a seat among the delegates for the rest of the meeting. Nobody, however, was elected to take his office. Even those who voted against him knew no one could take his place in the larger world as representative for the Jewish people.

The following spring, Chaim and Vera Weizmann returned to Rehovoth. Though in failing health, he worked in his laboratory there and busied himself with the building of the Weizmann Institute of Science. He spoke out often. When he heard that Jewish extremists had blown up a British Officers' Club, Dr. Weizmann insisted that terrorism harmed the Jewish cause.

As the British inability to rule effectively in Palestine became clearer, the British government referred the entire Palestine problem to the United Nations.

The United Nations appointed a Special Committee on Palestine to study the situation. This committee traveled in Europe and in the Middle East to collect information from the British, from Arabs, and from Jews. Once again Dr. Weizmann appeared before an investigating body in the Holy Land.

The committee recommended that the British give up their mandate, and that Palestine be partitioned into two separate and independent Jewish and Arab states. They also urged that Jerusalem become an international city.

While the United Nations considered the report, Chaim Weizmann rested in his Rehovoth home, trying to gather his strength for another operation on his eyes. A cable came from his Zionist colleagues asking him to go to America to help with the presentation of their case at the United Nations.

The doctor advised Dr. Weizmann not to make this trip, but the leader would not give up his life cause now. He and Vera returned to New York.

When Dr. Weizmann stood up in the United Nations, he appeared to many as an ancient Hebrew prophet. There was heroism in this aging, half-blind spokesman, who had crossed continents and oceans to convince the world's statesmen of the truth and justice of the Jewish cause. He tried to read his notes, but his poor eyesight made this impossible. He had to speak extemporaneously.

Dr. Weizmann said, "My mind goes back something like twenty-five years to the time when in the Council Chamber of the League of Nations a somewhat similar discussion took place." He enumerated the many broken pledges to his people, and how each broken promise had created more suspicion and hatred until all hope of peace had disappeared. "The Jews are entitled to a home of their own," he said, "but there will be benefits for our Arab neighbors; they will profit from Jewish work on the land."

The United Nations would discuss the partition proposal later. Dr. Weizmann went on to Washington, D.C., where President Truman received him cordially.

"If there is to be a division of the Negev Desert," Dr. Weizmann said, "that division should be vertical. It is imperative that Elath, the port on the Gulf of Aqaba, at the southern tip of the Negev, belong to the Jewish State. If the Egyptians choose to be hostile to us, which I hope will not be the case, they can close navigation to us through the Suez Canal. The Gulf of Aqaba would give us a path to the Far East."

President Truman studied the map of the Middle East and agreed with Dr. Weizmann. He promised to communicate with the American delegation at the United Nations right away. The vertical division of the Negev was more sensible.

Dr. Weizmann returned to his New York hotel worn and weary. On November 29, 1947, when the United Nations was scheduled to vote on the partition plan, he was too exhausted to attend the roll call. As he and Vera listened to the radio report, he broke down and sobbed with happiness and relief. The United Nations had voted 33 to 13 for partition and for the end of the British mandate.

The United Nations' resolution read as follows:

> The Mandate for Palestine shall terminate as soon as possible, but in any case not later than August first, 1948. . . . Independent Arab and Jewish states, and the specific international regime for the City of Jerusalem . . . shall come into existence in Palestine two months after the evacuation of the armed forces of the Mandatory Power has been completed, but in any case no later than October first, 1948.

Chaim and Vera Weizmann smiled tearfully at each other while the news spread like sudden sunshine throughout the world.

Dr. Weizmann was urged to join the crowds that gathered in the corridor outside his hotel room. In his happiness, he gathered his strength and accompanied his friends to a hall when tens of thousands of Jews had gathered spontaneously to celebrate. Masses of people were pushing into the great auditorium. Recognizing Chaim Weizmann, some young men lifted him on their shoulders, and bore him triumphantly through the crowd to the stage.

When Chaim Weizmann appeared on the platform, everyone burst out singing "Hatikvah," the Jewish song of hope. At last the hope had been fulfilled.

16. Birth of a Nation

With the U.N. vote for partition over, Dr. Weizmann thought his life work was completed. He and Vera took the first plane possible out of New York and flew to London for a joyful reunion with their son Benjy, Benjy's wife, and their grandson David. After a short stay, they intended to give up their home in London and move permanently to Palestine.

However, disturbing reports of British actions in Palestine soon arrived. The British, who were not in favor of the partition, hampered the Jews at every turn. The British administration was allowing irregular Arab forces to cross the Jordan River into Palestine, yet was arresting Haganah men as they tried to defend Jewish lives. The British would not protect the Jewish community, but they would not acknowledge the right of Jews to protect themselves either. They refused to pass on government services to their incoming Jewish successors; they even refused to permit the United Nations committee to enter Palestine. Under these circumstances, the Arabs increased their attacks on the Palestinian Jews.

Dr. Weizmann was anxious to get to Palestine; he believed he could be of service there. He and Vera were scheduled to fly there in the middle of January, but by that time he was receiving urgent phone calls from friends in the United States.

"You must return to the United States immediately," they told him. "The British are telling the U.N. that partition won't work. They want another vote on the recommendations of the Special Committee. We need you here."

"How are they persuading the members?" Dr. Weizmann asked.

"The British are pointing to the increased fighting in Palestine between the Arabs and the Jews," was the answer.

"The British do their best to keep us from defending ourselves and then complain that we are unable to do so," Dr. Weizmann sighed. "I will come." He hung up the receiver, turned to Vera, and said, "We have just left New York, but now we must go back. My work is not completed yet."

The Weizmanns repacked their bags, and returned to New York. It was early February 1948, and a blizzard swirled over the city.

There were many hectic consultations, meetings, and telephone calls. The activity and the miserable weather proved too much for Dr. Weizmann's fragile health. He became ill and had to rest in a darkened hotel room.

He got up from his sick bed, however, to go to Washington, D.C., to visit President Truman again. Truman was sympathetic and frank. He told Dr. Weizmann that he supported the partition plan.

Yet twenty-four hours later, the American ambassador to the United Nations spoke publicly against the partition; he was afraid of greater Arab uprisings as were some members of the United States State Department. The ambassador suggested another trusteeship for Palestine.

Dr. Weizmann, surprised and indignant, doubted that President Truman was aware of the American ambassador's statement. He wrote to the president.

"The choice for our people, Mr. President," Dr. Weizmann wrote, "is between statehood and extermination. History and Providence have placed this issue in your hands. I am confident that you will decide it in the spirit of the moral law."

Dr. Weizmann also issued a statement to the press:

> The plan worked out by the [U.N.] Assembly was the result of a long and careful process of deliberation in which the conflicting claims of the various parties were judged in the light of international equity. . . . We accepted . . . limitations only because they were decreed by the supreme authority of international judg-

ment, and because in the small area allotted to us we would be free to bring in our people, and enjoy the indispensable boon of sovereignty—a privilege conferred upon the Arabs in vast territories...

President Truman kept his word and continued to support the partition plan. This helped defeat those who were calling for a new vote and permitted the original vote favoring partition to stand.

While Dr. Weizmann was working in America, Ben Gurion and other Zionist leaders were busy in Palestine preparing a declaration of independence for their new nation and setting up a government. They were building an army and an air force and were preparing the country to receive thousands of Jewish refugees from the Displaced Persons' Camps of Europe and the British detention center on Cyprus.

Now that they had lost American backing, the British decided to end their mandate at midnight of May 14.

Dr. Weizmann cabled Palestinian leaders: "Declare a Jewish state the moment the British leave."

Eight hours before the British mandate was ended, the Jewish state was proclaimed by the National Council in Tel Aviv as the State of Israel. It would come into being as soon as the British mandate ended at midnight.

The flag of the proud new state flutters over its joyous citizens on Independence Day.

Dr. Weizmann smiled, and tears of joy flooded his eyes. Friends crowded into the hotel to congratulate him. They were still celebrating when an aide burst into his room. "Chief—," he started to say.

Before he could utter another word, Dr. Weizmann quickly said, "President Truman has recognized the State of Israel."

"How could you know?" the aide asked. "The message just came, and your radio is off."

"I saw it in your face," Dr. Weizmann said gently.

The next day brought a cablegram to Dr. Weizmann from Ben Gurion. It stated:

> On the occasion of the establishment of the Jewish State, we send our greetings to you, who have done more than any living man towards its creation. Your stand and help have strengthened all of us. We look forward to the day when we shall see you at the head of the State established in peace.

Dr. Weizmann was still smiling, with the cable in his hand, when a New York newspaper editor telephoned. Vera answered the phone.

"We have just received a cable dispatch from Tel Aviv," the editor said. "Dr. Weizmann has been chosen president of Israel. We would like to know how he feels about it."

Vera turned to her husband and said, "Congratulations, Chaimchik, you are now the president."

Dr. Weizmann looked up at his wife. "What nonsense is this?"

Vera repeated the editor's message. "You will undoubtedly receive a cable tomorrow," she added.

"Dr. Weizmann is very pleased," Vera told the editor, and hung up the receiver.

Actually Dr. Weizmann was so touched that he had

little to say. He whispered a blessing. History had spared a portion of the Jewish people so that they could taste the thrill of having their own independent country and a president of their own.

Soon the blue and white flag of Israel flew for the first time over the Weizmanns' hotel, but the news from Israel was bitter. The new nation was fighting for its life as Egyptian aircraft bombed Tel Aviv. Armies of six Arab states surrounding Israel were moving against the new nation. Former Nazi officers were helping them.

The kibbutzim, or agricultural communes, which had been established over the years by settlers in Palestine, proved to have been strategically placed. Many of them were used as forts to defend the new nation. Children were sent inland as Jews in the border settlements fought for land that the United Nations had granted them.

Amid the terrifying news, Dr. and Mrs. Weizmann traveled to Washington, D.C., where the aging leader sought President Truman's help once more.

Upon their arrival in the American capital, the Weizmanns were met by representatives of the State Department and the mayor of Washington. Crowds of people waving Israeli flags and singing "Hatikvah" lined the streets as they passed.

Press cameras flashed and newsreels whirred as the first president of Israel presented the thirty-third

The new president of Israel presents a Torah, in a velvet cover, to the president of the United States.

president of the United States with a Torah, the first five books of the Bible, hand lettered on parchment.

When the two presidents were alone, President Weizmann offered his thanks for President Truman's support. Then he asked that the United States' embargo on arms to the Middle East be lifted so that the new nation might buy weapons for defense.

"This is now under serious consideration," President Truman said.

"We will need a loan of $100,000,000 for defense and reconstruction," President Weizmann said.

"I don't see any difficulty in advancing the loan," President Truman answered.

Lastly, President Weizmann requested recognition for the Israeli ambassador.

"That will come in due course," President Truman replied.

The Weizmanns returned to New York and caught up with news from Palestine. The mufti was broadcasting instructions to Palestinian Arabs; he urged them to withdraw into Arab countries until the Jews were beaten and pushed into the sea. Then, he said, the Arabs could return and take over Jewish homes.

Although Israeli officials urged the Arabs to remain in their homes, many Arabs, fearful of the fighting, left Israel. Those who remained were given citizenship and opportunities to earn a living.

The war was still going on at the end of May when the Weizmanns left New York for Israel. They traveled via France and Switzerland. A plane bearing the blue and white flag of Israel came to Geneva to fly them home. They arrived in Israel the next morning at 5 A.M. Nevertheless, members of the government, friends, and relations met them at the airport and escorted them to breakfast.

After resting, President Weizmann visited war-torn Israeli border settlements to encourage the farmer–soldiers. At each kibbutz, he was told miraculous tales of tanks stopped at the very gate by homemade bombs and by settlers grabbing guns from the dead.

The war continued for nearly six months. The

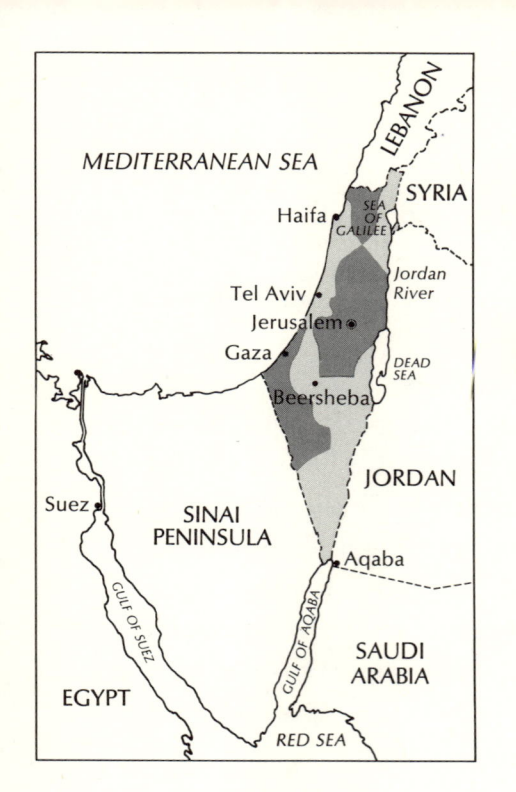

| | The portion of Palestine proposed as a Jewish state by the United Nations, 1948 |
| | The portion of Palestine proposed as an Arab state by the United Nations, 1948 |

| | The State of Israel at the end of the Arab-Israeli war, 1948–1949 |
| | Palestinian territory held by adjoining Arab states at the end of the Arab-Israeli war, 1948–1949 |

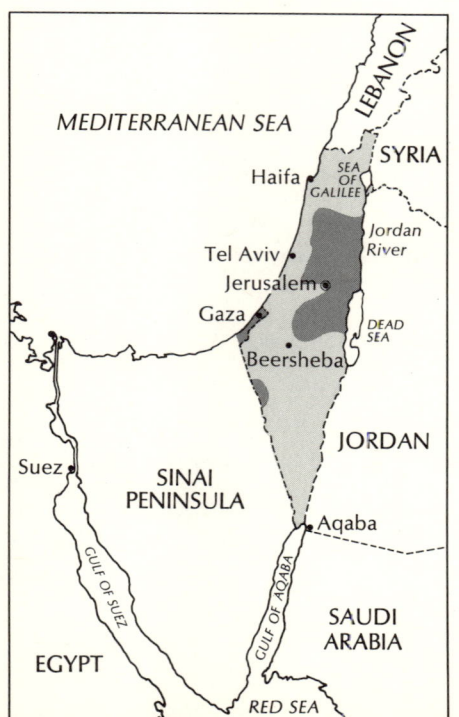

The United Nations' plan divided Palestine into two states — Jewish and Arab (above). After invading Arab armies were turned back, the boundaries of the new Jewish state of Israel were as shown at left.

Arab armies had better equipment and more men, but the Israelis were fighting for their very existence. The troops of each invading nation were turned back by the Haganah, by the valiant men of the kibbutz, and sometimes by the Irgun. Eventually the Israelis drove the Egyptians out of the Negev Desert and turned away the Iraqis, Jordanians, Syrians, and the Lebanese.

An armistice signed with the Egyptians was followed by similar agreements with Lebanon, Jordan, and Syria. Iraq refused to sign an armistice because she had no common border with Israel.

With the enemy driven out, the young State of Israel scheduled a general election for January 25, 1949. The Knesset, or parliament, was to be elected by the Israelis in a system of proportional representation. This system insured representation in the Knesset for every section of the population, including the Arabs. Indeed, Israel became the first country in which Arab women attained the vote.

Chaim Weizmann was officially named by the Knesset as the first president of Israel. He was to serve much as the French president, in a position of great honor, while the prime minister did the work.

President Weizmann's first official function was to call upon the newly elected prime minister David Ben Gurion and ask him to form a cabinet. A few weeks later, on February 14, 1949, President Weizmann opened the Knesset in Jerusalem.

As President Chaim Weizmann entered the assembly hall to open the Knesset, the sound of the ram's horn, Israel's ancient instrument, echoed. President Weizmann stood erect as he took the oath of office. Then he gave a speech stressing Israel's ancient ethical foundations and his hope for peace with the Arabs:

> This day is a great day in our lives. Let us not be thought too arrogant if we say that it is also a great day in the history of the world. At this hour a message of hope and good cheer goes forth from this place, from this sacred city, to all those throughout the world who are persecuted and oppressed, and who are struggling for freedom and equality. A just struggle is indeed of avail. If we, the people of sorrows and affliction, have been vouchsafed this event of today, then truly there is hope at the end for all who long for justice.

On March 1, President Weizmann made his first official visit to Tel Aviv. Some 150,000 people crowded the streets, balconies, and roof tops. Gaily colored banners hung out of the windows, and children fluttered the blue and white Israeli flags.

Back at his Rehovoth home, President Weizmann

Chaim Weizmann casts a vote at Israel's first national election and, at right, is sworn in as the president of the new state.

often visited the nearly completed Weizmann Institute of Science. He hoped this scientific institute would become a leading research center for the entire Middle East. In Jerusalem, the Hebrew University was offering courses in the humanities, science, law, medicine, and agriculture. All parts of Israel were served by agricultural experiment stations. Agriculture, as Chaim Weizmann foretold many years before, remained a basic science in Israel.

President Weizmann visited many schools where free education was available for all children. While Hebrew was the official language, the teachers of Arab schools taught in Arabic. Israeli law insured freedom of worship for all faiths, giving no church special legal privileges, for there were thousands of Moslems and Christians in the land.

Israel was at last a nation, but President Weizmann's work was not yet finished. There were several more tasks to carry out. He let himself be persuaded to attend a fund-raising dinner in New York for the Weizmann Institute of Science.

This meant he had to be in New York on the first anniversary of Israel's independence. A tremendous crowd of American Jews and friends of Israel gathered in Madison Square Garden to hear Israel's first president speak.

When President Weizmann entered the vast hall, 150,000 people stood up, cheering and clapping, in a tribute to the aged leader. Tired and worn, he sensed that this was his last trip to the United States.

Back in Israel, Chaim and Vera drove to Jerusalem on August 17, 1949, to attend reinterment ceremonies for Theodor Herzl. In his will, Herzl had asked that the "Jewish people... carry my remains to the State of Israel." Now he was laid to rest on a ridge facing Jerusalem. The hill was renamed Mount Herzl.

In November, on President Weizmann's seventy-fifth birthday, the Weizmann Institute of Science was formally dedicated in Rehovoth. An impressive assembly of Israeli and foreign scientists gathered and heard Prime Minister Ben Gurion describe the president as "a man to whom it has fallen to be adorned with two crowns, the crown of statesmanship and the crown of learning."

That same year, 1949, Weizmann's autobiography, *Trial and Error,* was published. The two volumes recounted the story of his life from its beginning in Motol in the previous century.

Two years later, on his seventy-seventh birthday, Chaim Weizmann received a note from Winston Churchill. The note read, "The wonderful exertions which Israel is making in these times of difficulty are cheering to an old Zionist like me. I trust you may work in with Jordan and the rest of the Moslem world. With true comradeship, there will be enough for all. Every good wish, my old friend."

Soon afterward, President Weizmann became desperately ill. For the entire year that followed, he had to stay in bed. Although he was extremely weak, his mind remained remarkably lucid. Vera seldom left his side.

Early on November 9, 1952, Chaim Weizmann, Israel's first president, died peacefully. The people of Israel and Jews throughout the world wept as though they had lost a personal friend, for his work and journeys were known among the poorest.

President Weizmann lay in state before his Rehovoth home for two days. Members of the Israeli armed forces stood guard at his bier as people from all walks of life came to pay their last respects. Prime Minister Ben Gurion bowed his head in sadness as he led the funeral procession.

Chaim Weizmann was buried in Rehovoth, within sight of the mountains of Judah, in the ancient land of his ancestors.

Chaim Weizmann's lifetime devotion to the Jewish national home lives on "in every kibbutz, in every inch of Israel's soil, in the Hebrew University, the Weizmann Institute of Science, and in the face of every wandering Jew who had settled at last in his ancient Home," it was said. After a lifetime of work for Zionism, Chaim Weizmann was home to stay.

Chronological List of Events in Chaim Weizmann's Life

1874 Chaim Weizmann is born on November 17 in the town of Motol in the Russian Pale of Settlement.

1878 Young Chaim goes to Pinsk to attend the Real-Gymnasium and becomes active there in the Zionist movement.

1892 Chaim leaves Russia for Germany to attend the University of Darmstadt and, later, the Polytechnium in Berlin.

1897 The first Zionist Congress meets in Basel, Switzerland, in 1897. It endorses Theodor Herzl's aim of building a Jewish state.

1900 After receiving a doctorate in chemistry, Dr. Weizmann takes a position at the University of Geneva as a lecturer. In Geneva he organizes several Zionist societies.

1903 In August Dr. Weizmann attends the sixth Zionist Congress, where Theodor Herzl announces the British offer of Uganda as a Jewish homeland.

1904 In July Dr. Weizmann moves to England, where he plans to live and continue his work in chemistry. He joins the faculty of Victoria University in Manchester. He is saddened by Herzl's death.

1906 Chaim Weizmann and Vera Chatzman are married in August in Zoppot, Germany.

1907   Dr. Weizmann visits Palestine for the first time. He continues to teach at Victoria University and becomes a leader of English Zionists.

1916   Dr. Weizmann offers his process for making acetone, which is used in the production of gunpowder, to the British during World War I. He then supervises the production of acetone.

1917   On November 2, the historic Balfour Declaration promises Jews a national home in Palestine.

1917   Dr. Weizmann has a friendly meeting with Emir Feisal. While he is in Palestine, ground is broken for the Hebrew University in Jerusalem.

1920   In San Remo, Italy, the victorious Allies give the British a mandate to govern Palestine in accordance with the Balfour Declaration.

1920   Dr. Weizmann becomes president of the World Zionist Organization.

1922   The British government issues the Churchill White Paper, affirming the Balfour Declaration but decreasing the area in which it applies.

1925   The opening ceremonies of Hebrew University take place in Jerusalem on April 1.

1930   The British government issues the Passfield White Paper. After a heated debate at the Zionist Congress of 1930, Dr. Weizmann resigns from the presidency. Arab protests against Jewish immigration and attacks on Jewish settlers increase throughout the 1930s.

1933   The Nazi party comes to power in Germany, and Adolph Hitler becomes chancellor. German Jews are beaten and jailed by his government.

1939   The British White Paper of 1939, slashing Jewish immigration to Palestine to 75,000 in five years and stopping the sale of land to Jews, is issued. It cuts off Palestine as a refuge for German Jews.

1939   In August, World War II begins. As Hitler's armies sweep across Europe, Jews in the conquered countries are sent to Nazi death camps.

1945   At the conclusion of World War II, it is discovered that six million Jews have been killed by the Nazis. Thousands of desperate survivors seek refuge in Palestine and are excluded by the White Paper of 1939. The British refer the Palestine problem to the United Nations.

1947   On November 29, the United Nations votes for the partition of Palestine and the end of the mandate.

1948   The State of Israel is established on May 14, and Chaim Weizmann is named president of the new nation.

1948   The armies of surrounding Arab nations invade the new nation of Israel immediately after its establishment. They are defeated in late 1948.

1952   On November 9, Chaim Weizmann, Israel's first president, dies at Rehovoth, Israel.

Index

A

Arabs, 36, 71-72, 92-93, 95-96, 103-108, 113-114, 118, 122-124, 129-133, 135, 137, 149-156, 158, 161, 163, 165-166, 168

B

Balfour, Arthur James, 63, 64 (pic), 65, 82, 84-86, 88-89, 91, 118-119, 120 (pic), 121
Balfour Declaration, 90-94, 108-111, 115-116, 124-125, 135
Ben Gurion, David, 93-94, 125, 137, 146, 150, 158, 160, 165, 169-170
Bevin, Ernest, 146
British
 administration of Palestine, 108, 109, 115-117, 123-125, 130-131, 135, 140-141
 interest in Zionism, 53, 54, 56, 57, 64, 84, 85, 86-91
 policy in Middle East, 85, 93, 122, 143
 Uganda offer, 53, 54, 56
 White Papers, 115-116, 124-125, 135-137, 140-141, 143, 145-146, 149
Buber, Martin, 47 (pic), 48

C

Chamberlain, Neville, 134-137, 139
Chatzman, Vera (Mrs. Chaim Weizmann). See Weizmann, Vera
Churchill White Paper of 1922, 115-116
Churchill, Winston, 79-80, 82-83, 85, 87 (pic), 88, 116, 139, 141, 143, 145, 169

D

Darmstadt, University of, 31-32
Detention Center (Cyprus), 148
Displaced Persons' Camps, 145, 148-149, 158

E

Einstein, Albert, 113, 123
Eisenberg, Aaron, 27, 29, 73-75, 128
English Zionist Federation, 87

F

Feisal, Emir, 93, 95-96, 97 (pic), 103-104, 116

H

Haganah, 114, 123, 130, 155, 165
 aid to refugees, 141, 147 (pic), 148
Haifa, 73, 105, 107, 148
Haj Amin el Husseini, 105-108, 113-114, 123, 129-130, 132-133
"Hatikvah," 40, 98, 154, 161
Hebrew University, 40, 42, 97-98, 111, 117-119, 121, 168, 170
Herzl, Theodor, 35-36, 37 (pic), 40-41, 44, 48, 51, 53, 55-58, 62, 112, 169
Hitler, Adolf, 127-128, 135-137, 149
Holy Land. See Palestine

I

Irgun Zvai Leumi, 130, 148, 165
Israel, 11, 71, 158, 159 (pic), 160, 161, 163, 165-166, 168-170

J

Jerusalem, 11-12, 16-17, 56, 65, 66, 73, 75, 84, 92, 96-98, 105-108, 114, 117-119, 123, 128, 144, 148, 152, 154, 165, 169
Jewish Agency, 122-124, 146
Jewish Brigade, 144
Jewish Colonial Trust, 42
Jewish National Fund, 111
Jewish National Home, 85, 88, 90, 110-111, 113, 116, 118, 122-123, 126, 170
Jewish State, The, 35-36, 51

K

Kishinev, 52-53, 55
Knesset, 165-166

L

Lawrence, T. E., 95-96
Lenin, Vladimir Ilyitch, 45-48, 84
Lloyd George, David, 85, 87 (pic), 99-100
"Lovers of Zion," 27, 29

M

MacDonald, Ramsay, 124-125
Manchester, Zionist Society, 62-63
Middle East, 72, 85, 93, 96, 133, 137, 151, 153, 162, 168
Montagu, Sir Edwin, 87-89
Moslems, 28, 98, 106, 123, 133, 168-169
Mosque of Omar, 28, 106-107, 123
Motol, 7, 8 (pic), 10, 14-15, 18-20, 22-23, 26, 34, 169

N

Nazis, 127-128, 131-134, 136-137, 139-142, 144, 148, 150, 161
Negev Desert, 153, 165

P

Pale of Settlement, 13 (pic), 14, 18, 22, 30, 38-39, 50, 84, 101
Palestine
   British administration of, 108, 109, 115-117, 123-125, 130-131, 135, 140-141
   conflict between Arabs and Jews, 105-108, 114-115, 122-123, 129 (pic), 130-133, 135, 137, 155, 163
   as Holy Land, 11-12, 16, 28, 29, 58, 78, 92, 102
   Jewish settlers in, 27, 36, 39-40, 48, 53-56, 62, 64, 74 (pic), 84-86, 88-91, 92-96, 101, 102 (pic), 104, 109-110, 128, 131, 134-135, 140-141, 145-151, 161
   partition of, 116, 151-152, 154-158
   Turkish rule of, 28, 37, 54, 72, 85-86, 91-93, 95, 141

Passfield White Paper of 1930, 124-125
Peel Report, 130-132, 135
Perkin, William Henry (Prof.), 58-60, 77
Pfungstadt, 31-32, 34, 88, 113
Pinsk, 18-22, 24, 26-27, 29-30, 34, 38, 52-53, 62, 73, 78, 91
Plekhanov, George, 45-48
Pogroms, 21-22, 52-53, 55, 106-108
Pomerantz, Maidie (Mrs. Benjamin Weizmann). See Weizmann, Maidie

R

Real-Gymnasium, 18-23, 30, 34, 43
Rehovoth, 73, 143, 150-152, 166, 169-170
Russia, Jewish life in, 10, 13-14, 18, 21-23, 26-27, 52-53, 84, 87

S

Samuel, Sir Herbert, 88, 109

T

Tel Aviv, 147, 158, 160-161
Trial and Error, 169
Truman, Harry S., 149, 153, 157-159, 161, 162 (pic), 163

U

Uganda, 53-56, 58, 62-64, 131
United Nations, 151-157, 161
United States, 83-84, 101, 162

V

Victoria University, 58, 60-61, 76

W

Weizmann, Benjamin (son), 70, 76, 79, 99, 105, 107-108, 117, 133, 137, 138 (pic), 142, 155
Weizmann, Chaim
   and acetone production, 68, 79-84, 100-101

and Balfour Declaration, 85-91, 92-93, 108, 109
childhood of, 7, 8 (pic), 9-11, 14-17
death of, 170
and early Zionist activities, 27, 29, 36-38, 39, 40, 46-48, 50-51
and founding of State of Israel, 158-159
in Geneva, 43-46, 47 (pic), 48-56
in Germany, 32-34, 35-37, 39-40, 42-43
and Hebrew University, 96-98, 117-119, 120 (pic), 121
and Jewish Agency, 122-123
marriage of, 66-67
in Palestine, 71-75, 92-93, 94 (pic), 95-96, 97 (pic), 98, 101-102, 117-121, 143-144
and Passfield White Paper, 124-125
and Peel Report, 130, 131, 132
in Pinsk, 21-23, 25 (pic), 26-27, 29
as president of Israel, 160-163, 165, 166, 167 (pic), 168-170
as president of World Zionist Organization, 109, 126, 128, 151
in Rehovoth, 128-129, 143, 150, 151, 152
and Uganda offer, 53-56
and United Nations, 152-154
in United States, 111-113, 141, 143, 152, 154, 156-163
at University of Freiberg, 42-43
at Victoria University, Manchester, 58-59, 60 (pic), 61, 67-68, 76-77, 78
and Weizmann Institute of Science, 149-150
and White Paper of 1939, 135, 137, 143, 145-146, 149
and Zionist Commission, 91, 92
and Zionist Congresses, 37, 38, 39, 40, 41, 42, 53-56, 62, 71, 109-110, 125-126, 131-133, 136, 150-151
Weizmann, David (grandson), 155
Weizmann, Feivel (brother), 7, 9, 19-23, 26, 66, 104, 107
Weizmann Institute of Science, 150-151, 168-170

Weizmann, Maidie (Mrs. Benjamin), 133, 142, 155
Weizmann, Maria (sister), 9, 34
Weizmann, Michael (son), 82, 99, 126, 137, 138 (pic), 139, 142-143
Weizmann, Miriam (sister), 66
Weizmann, Oser (father), 7, 9, 14-15, 17-19, 30-31, 34, 39, 41-43, 55, 66, 77
Weizmann, Rachel (mother), 7, 9-10, 16-17, 29, 42-43, 66, 78, 104, 107
Weizmann, Shemuel (brother), 55
Weizmann, Vera (Mrs. Chaim), 49-52, 57-59, 66-69, 70 (pic), 75-78, 82, 88, 99, 101-103, 111-112, 117, 126, 128, 133, 137, 139, 142-143, 151-156, 160-161, 169-170
White Papers
of 1922 (Churchill), 115-116
of 1930 (Passfield), 124-125
of 1939, 135-137, 140-141, 143, 145-146, 149
World War I, 79-84, 85-86, 99-101
World War II, 134-145
World Zionist Organization, 103, 110, 124, 126, 128, 151

Z

Zion. *See* Palestine
Zionism, 27, 39, 44-45, 47, 50-52, 54, 57-58, 63, 67, 70, 73, 84, 86, 88, 90-92, 101, 104, 108, 110, 113, 115, 117, 122, 125-126, 130, 150, 169-170
Zionist Commission, 91-98
Zionist Congresses, 48, 51, 111, 125
First, 36-40
Second, 39, 41-42
Sixth, 53-56, 58, 64
Seventh, 62
Eighth, 71
Twelfth, 109-110
Twentieth, 131-132
Twenty-First, 136
Twenty-Second, 150